"Reading this book feels like sitting down get their clear-eyed take on what's limiting your thinking. It has already changed the way I think about work and leadership. With clarity and compassion, Mettler and Yarian will rattle the cage of what you think you already understand. But beware: if you read it, it will certainly spark your curiosity; if you apply it, it will change your life."

J. Ross Blankenship, PhD, author of
Assessing CEOs and Senior Leaders:
A Primer for Consultants

"Jon Yarian is the flint I strike against when I need inspiration, and *Spark* is the perfect distillation of his approach. I'm stoked to have Jon and Chris' guidebook handy whenever I need help unlocking my most productive, essential power."

Stanfield Gray, Founder & CEO, Dig South

"Chris Mettler and Jon Yarian have written an outstanding book on business and leadership. Whether you are just starting your career or sitting comfortably in the CEO's suite you must read this book. The authors clearly identify important and easily understood concepts that drive success in organizations and people. They also provide in detail the steps to take along the way to realize you have embraced and implemented these concepts. Unlike so many of these books which are filled with jargon, this book is a crisp, warm and caring conversation with two very successful, humble, and self-aware entrepreneurs. The book will transform the way you go about your work, but it provides even more to the reader. It could have just as easily been titled '24 Concepts to Ignite, Unstick or Supercharge your Personal Life!' Read this book and dedicate yourself to following its path forward. It will pay you back in many professional ways, and it will also have an equal impact on your personal life. A truly new and important contribution to the field!"

Nicholas S. Zeppos, Vanderbilt University
Chancellor Emeritus Chair

SPARK

24 Concepts to Ignite, Unstick or Supercharge Your Work Life

CHRIS METTLER & JON YARIAN

BLOOMSBURY BUSINESS
LONDON • OXFORD • NEW YORK • NEW DELHI • SYDNEY

BLOOMSBURY BUSINESS
Bloomsbury Publishing Plc
50 Bedford Square, London, WC1B 3DP, UK
29 Earlsfort Terrace, Dublin 2, Ireland

BLOOMSBURY, BLOOMSBURY BUSINESS and the Diana logo are trademarks
of Bloomsbury Publishing Plc

First published in Great Britain 2023

A catalogue record for this book is available from the British Library

Library of Congress Cataloguing-in-Publication data has been applied for

ISBN: 978-1-3994-0761-8; eBook: 978-1-3994-0758-8

4 6 8 10 9 7 5

Typeset by Deanta Global Publishing Services, Chennai, India
Printed and bound in U.S.A.

To find out more about our authors and books visit www.bloomsbury.com
and sign up for our newsletters

This book is dedicated to our partners, Kate Mettler and Melissa Ellis-Yarian, without whom this project (and many other things) would not have been possible. We dedicate it to our children (Chris: Lucy, Molly, Grady and Cam; Jon: Eamon and Joanna), who are worth every effort to make the world a better place. We also honor our parents, siblings, teachers, and others that sacrificed to give us a better chance at whole and happy lives.

Coach Toby Simpson is owed a debt of gratitude for inspiring Chris to move from idea to action and get the project started. Special thanks are owed to Victoria Kelly, David Fouse and the team at Pinkston whose leadership moved this from a messy manuscript to the real deal. Thanks to Heike Schussler for the incredible cover design and her willingness to work with us long before there was any assurance of publication. We appreciate Ian Hallsworth, Allie Collins, Jane Donovan and everyone else at Bloomsbury for believing in us and giving the book a chance to find an audience.

Finally, we acknowledge all our colleagues at Sovereign Co and each of our investee companies, now and to come, for the privilege of learning from them every single day.

Contents

Introductions

No one ever thought I would run my own company, never mind write a book. I grew up with mild dyslexia. Until I was 12, my mother would drive me an hour each way, three times per week, so I could work with a reading specialist. My mother never owned a company or sat inside a boardroom, but she is still one of the best examples of selfless leadership I've ever known—many of the concepts in this book began by learning from my parents. They believed in hard work and taught me to "carry the water". Leaders who don't participate in the labor lose touch with who and what they manage.

I barely got into Vanderbilt University for undergrad, and I tested six times to finally get the lowest score acceptable for entrance at Northwestern University's Kellogg School of Management. There were many long-suffering professors and classmates who were skeptical that I would find success after graduation.

This book is for anyone who had to be resilient and tap into the fire (or inferno!) inside of them to overcome a challenge. It's for those who aren't finding purpose in bloated organizations, who don't like to hold meetings for meetings' sake, and who want to live each day as their last, instead of just getting through. We wrote the book in short chapters so readers could find value in short bursts. It's written in everyday language and offers examples that real people can relate to. In short, we wrote it for people like me. Our aim for this book is that it helps you overcome whatever obstacles stand between you and the life you want to live.

Chris Mettler

I grew up pretending to know what I was doing. My brothers and I were homeschooled and moved frequently. We were very close, and I was determined to be included with them in whatever they were up to. That made me always the youngest and least prepared. Add to it the necessity of making new friends every three or four years and before too long, I got pretty good at acting the part. I learned how to seem older, nod like I understood, appear not just qualified but cocky. It helped me get along and it deprived me of a lot of opportunities to learn. After all, you can't ask questions if your goal is to seem like you already know the answers.

Years later, having become masterful at pretending, I began to wonder what (if anything) I really knew. I had been using words like leadership, power, and purpose all my life and part of me felt like a parrot: I knew how to reproduce the sound but had no concept of its meaning. A series of generous mentors helped me along. A few mistakes, some of them costly, taught me great lessons as well. I became an entrepreneur and discovered that most people don't know what they are talking about either— that helped me feel better. The answer for me, ultimately, was to become the opposite of how I behaved as a kid: I learned to ask dumb questions, risk embarrassment, and embrace failure for the gift of knowledge it offers.

This book is for anyone afraid of getting found out for being the frauds they are. It's for the pretenders, the fit-in folks, the people of all ages who sacrificed learning in order to be included. There is nothing wrong with wanting to belong or be accepted but sooner or later, the time comes when we need answers of our own. Principles that guide us or at least an active definition of what we are doing and how to measure it. There is no greater example of one's willingness to run the risk of being wrong than writing a book. I'm certain I am wrong, often, and that many readers will catch me and point out the flaws in what you are about to read. And I'll learn from that, too.

The point is not to avoid failure, it's to earn knowledge and move with purpose no matter the cost. I hope this book helps someone find their path a little sooner than I did.

Jon Yarian

Preface

This isn't a book. You might be reading it. You might even be holding a bound collection of pressed wood pulp, looking down at what you thought was one of the first pages of a book. But our intention was never to create a "book," because doing so would mean you are influenced by what you think a book should be, what you might expect from a book, or whether or not it sounds bookish enough. For example, outside of our introductions, we never mention ourselves or our careers. This is completely intentional. All of the concepts have been tested successfully in the companies we've built, but if we really believe that true leadership is selfless, then we would be hypocrites to write a book about ourselves.

Don't think of this as a book. Think of it as a conversation.

This conversation we're about to have, the one we've invited you to join, is about approaching your career, business at large, and life itself from a perspective that is present and curious and creative. It is a philosophy that has no room for presupposing or assuming anything. It doesn't include making anything to be like other things or to fit in or be safe.

You might find it to be beneficial to read the chapters in order but we like to think of this more like a playlist than a linear narrative. Some of you may find more benefit by un-booking the experience for yourselves and letting the ideas bounce around.

If nothing else, we ask that you don't think you already know what you are about to experience. That presumption will rob you of all curiosity, color the way you hear what we have to say, and leave you right where you started: inside of a world that behaves according to the rules you have already decided on.

Unfortunately, many of you *still think this is a book* despite what we've just said. That's because you think you know what a book is, and it is safer to sit with what you think you know then face the possibilities and consequences of what you don't know. That space—what you don't know—is where your success lives. Moving into what you don't know with the courage to explore and learn is what will lead you to start a new business, grow the one you have, be a better leader, and ultimately, make the dent in the universe you've dreamed about.

In addition to your open-mindedness and curiosity, we ask for your commitment. Right now, you may be thinking, *This looks interesting, so I'll give it a shot. I'll start it and see where it goes.* A lot of people who read books are committed to less than 10 minutes of effort before they bail out. If this doesn't grab you by then, it's over. From a financial perspective, you have probably invested a few pounds or dollars. To many of you, it wasn't very much and you wouldn't notice if it simply vanished from your bank account. But let's look at something larger. Let's take a look at your work, whatever you do to earn money and provide for yourself and whomever depends on you. For many of you, your commitment to your work isn't all that different from your commitment to this conversation: *You are seeing how it goes.* You started it, you don't hate it, it compensates you well enough, you've been doing it for a while, you are (reasonably) good at it, and here we are. The Bermuda Triangle of non-commitment. Or just committed enough to maintain the status quo. This kind of approach will get you to the next page. It will get you to the next paycheck. But it won't get you what you really want.

Now look at the areas of your life where you've given your maximum commitment—actions, relationships, anything where you see yourself as really and truly committed. You'll notice that true commitment is often spoken out loud. It is declared and known and understood and other people *work around it*. It reshapes your environment and makes things different.

We are asking for you to commit yourself to this conversation and already know, before going any further, that you are going to test it out. If you take the time to read/listen and come across something new (remember, be open to the possibility that you don't already know everything), we want you to commit to using it in your life to see how it works. Think of it as a road test—drive the car around for a minute and see how you like it.

What matters is your action, your energy, your forward motion. You get no points for simply "finishing" this, telling yourself that you get it and staying safe inside your own assumptions and uncommitted approach to work and life. The magic of this conversation occurs when you apply it. When change occurs in your career and momentum is created toward bigger and better things. We want you to believe that this is entirely possible for you.

Will you allow it to happen?

The Structure of this Book

We're excited to present you with a (mostly) modular book, something you can read in almost any order and still be able to understand. We think of the chapters almost like songs on a playlist and expect our readers to rearrange, mark their favorites, and recommend to others in whatever order they prefer. With all of that said, we did want to offer some guidance in how we thought you might experience the ideas that follow.

Section One includes concepts that you can consider and work on *within yourself*. They require choice and commitment, but not the participation of other people. In many ways, these are the most challenging to master as they can require a level of self-examination and honesty that most of us would prefer to avoid. Gaining an understanding of each of these concepts, if not mastery, is extremely useful when we need to consider our behavior in relation to others.

Section Two includes concepts that would show up in *interpersonal relationships*. These concepts are very relevant in work partnerships, co-founder relationships, small project or department teams, or anywhere that two people need to produce results *together*. They can be understood on your own but only really applied with another person.

Section Three includes concepts that could be *shared across entire organizations*. If modeled and explained, they could become a part of company culture, the very atmosphere of groups that we often take for granted. These concepts are interested in group dynamics and situations where teams of people must act together in order to make things happen.

Most concepts reference or rely on other concepts, and there is certainly some overlap and gray area between them. This leads us to the fourth and final section, the only part of the book that presupposes one has already read the rest of the book. **Section Four** includes *combinations and sequences of concepts*, ways that they naturally lead or lend themselves to each other. Maximizing the value of this section requires some serious consideration of what came before and an intention to move into a more challenging level of engagement.

Are there other concepts that could have been included? Of course. Will some readers notice combinations we neglected to include, find a concept they feel is a better fit for another tier? Certainly. Use our organization model if it serves your experience, and feel free to customize and upgrade as you see fit. We're excited to be in the conversation with you and know that it will benefit from your perspective.

Chris and Jon

Concepts you work on within yourself

The foundations of this book are concepts that can change the way you think about yourself and in doing so, make possible the change you want to create in the world. The following chapters will ask you, in a variety of ways, to reconsider how you see yourself and what is possible for your life. To be sure, only you can create this change. This book will not change you from the outside-in. We only hope to be the spark that initiates change, a part of the process that results in a much bigger vision for what you can accomplish and what it means to be you.

To get the most out of this first section, try to set aside everything you think you already know about words like "leadership," "power," "purpose," and the rest of the ideas we'll discuss. Be open to the possibility that these words could hold new meaning moving forward, definitions that can guide you in real life. Try them out and see if they work. It's all we can ask. We're glad you're here and see unlimited potential in your power to create.

CHAPTER ONE

Leadership

Take a moment to list everything of which you truly consider yourself to be in charge. Everything that you really, actually, direct and control. Set aside your ability to move your body, make noises, or anything that falls into the category of mind-body governance. What are we left with?

If you were really in charge of your team at work, things would be very different. You are a part of your friendship group, and occasionally direct them to a restaurant or bar, but you are far from being the boss of any of them. It's possible you experience your home life as the opposite of being in charge—many of you may feel like an underappreciated employee of your spouse and kids. Even your pets remind you on a regular basis that control is an illusion and on any given day, a rug can get ruined for no apparent reason.

What do we make of this? How do we reconcile it with our experience of people who do, in fact, appear to be in control of things? How was that control created? How is it maintained?

In order to get closer to the answer, we have to explode the myth of control. A *lack of control* is actually just part of the human experience. There is nothing wrong with you. Desiring control is natural and normal, and hoping to be seen as "in control" is present in all of us. However, when we act from a place of seeking control, we are quickly reminded how little of it we possess. This brings us to a concept called leadership but before we go any further, get rid of everything you think you know about leadership. Leadership is one of the most misunderstood and overused terms in any language, and it's often just used as code for people who seek to control or hope to be seen as being in control of something—that's not real leadership.

Remember, desiring control is natural and normal and hoping to be seen as "in control" is present in all of us. The only problem is that it doesn't produce useful results.

The search for control is all about you—what *you* want to be different or better or just more to your liking. Being seen as "in control" is driven by self-image—how you desire to be seen and experienced by others. It's a closed loop of you thinking about you, even when you consciously connect it to "growing the company" or "getting the house organized" or even "getting the dog to stop @&$%ing on the rug."

Leadership is the relinquishment of the illusion of control. It is the willingness to be seen for who you really are, and the commitment to serve others in search of a goal greater than yourself.

Whew! Lots happening there. Let's break that down in sections:

1) Relinquishment of the illusion of control.

    This means you already know you aren't in control, and you have achieved a level of peace with it (not that it won't bother you from time to time or require conscious effort to manage). The impulse to control and be seen as being in control is very powerful though and will never totally go away. See it for what it is and work through it.

    Having set it aside, it will be easier for you to dispense with a bunch of other stuff that doesn't align with true leadership.

This includes coercion ("Do it, or else!"), bribery ("If I pay you enough, will you do it my way?"), disengagement with others ("I'll do it myself!"), etc. These come from the control impulse and pop up in all kinds of cleverly disguised ways. Most meetings in most offices all around the world are conversations about the application of control through one or more of these methodologies.

Getting a handle on your desire for control and the unhelpful urges it produces is the essential first step to having others experience you as a leader. Consider it, work on it, and do not proceed beyond it until you have it in hand, because nothing will work if you bring a desire to control along with you.

2) Willingness to be seen for who you really are.
In order to get to what we mean here, you'll have to be open to the possibility that no one is fooling nearly as many people as they think they are. Over time, a desire to control comes across to others, and they will react accordingly, defending themselves from the toxic effects it produces.

Consider everyone you've ever worked for and think about how obvious it was to everyone when your "leader" was obsessed with being in control and/or looking like they had control. Now consider the effect it had on you—did those individuals get the best out of you? Did they unlock your complete and utter full potential? It's possible they produced some very short-term results because they had the opportunity to make people stay late or pay them more for better results but you wouldn't call it true leadership.

If we're setting aside the desire to control (*see* Step 1), what's left for people to see in you? Your commitment to them and your vision for what is possible for you to accomplish together.

They will also clearly see your knowledge gaps and deficiencies, the fact that you need them to get where you want to go, etc. Most of us are nervous about these vulnerabilities. That's normal. Just remind yourself that anyone you hope to lead can see them anyways so lean into it. Be who you are. Connect with them from a place of commitment instead of control. Which brings us to...

3) Commitment to serve others in search of a goal greater than yourself.

Can you see how we're taking you out of the equation? Can you feel the "you" coming out of the process as we focus on them (the folks you hope to lead) and the goal (where you will get to together)? We've landed in a place that overlaps with much of the rest of the conversation, and you can skip around to a number of other sections from here (Power, Co-creation, Accountability, Scalability, etc.).

For now, we want to focus on the possibility of something greater than yourself. This can be a challenging issue for anyone engaged in work or involved in relationships that don't inspire them. Maybe setting aside control and being willing to be seen for who you really are exposes some contradictions in your life. That's okay! It can be the first step toward changing the things that will unlock you as a real leader. Or this process could lead to the realization of how badly you want to launch a startup, ship a product, grow your department, etc. By setting aside the fear of failure and personal insecurity, you have discovered an authentic desire to get someplace. This desire— the identification of a goal greater than yourself—is the thing you need help with and in order to get the best help, you'll have to serve the people you need to get there.

This means understanding them as unique individuals, honestly considering the conditions and circumstances that would set them up for success, defending them against distractions and bureaucracy, rewarding them generously, and giving them all the credit they deserve. After all, you don't control them! You actually *need* them to get anywhere. When you work from a place of serving them, you create an environment where they see your goal as their goal and things actually start to get done. The corporate blob begins to move in a more efficient direction.

Our definition of leadership often *feels like* vulnerability, service, trust, and a desire for something bigger than (and entirely separate from) yourself. What it *looks like* to others is the person they want to, and are inspired to, follow; someone they would describe as an authentic leader. Let's go back to your memories of everyone you've ever worked for—can you find any leaders in there? Think about school, social groups, other environments. The authentic leaders stand out, and the more you look at them, the more you will likely come to realize that they were there for you in service of something bigger so you decided to buy in and *together*, you made things happen. That is real leadership.

CHAPTER TWO

Purpose

If you've ever played poker or bet on sports, it's likely you are familiar with a feeling that has been dubbed the "gambler's fallacy". Simply put, it holds that if a particular event occurs more frequently than normal during the past, it is less likely to happen in the future (or the reverse). If one of your opponents has been drawing all the best cards, you will eventually be the one getting them. Your fantasy football players have underperformed for weeks, so you are due for a big Sunday.

Even if you've never bet a dollar in your life, you have probably encountered this phenomenon. It's rooted in the expectation that your turn is coming; karma evens everything out; what goes around comes around; and your day will come. Except that it might not. The gambler's fallacy is flatly, obviously wrong—that's why they call it a fallacy. The truth is that the odds are the same every time. The universe is random. It's possible you never get the good cards, your team just keeps losing, and your day never comes.

This false but familiar feeling is one of the most common ways we compensate in order to deal with failure. Unable to accept it for what it is—a big, fat lie—we instantly and unconsciously search for explanations that remove blame and create false hope.

As any decent card player will tell you, waiting for "good" cards is not a winning strategy. If your horses lose all the time, you probably aren't very adept at picking them. Gambling, for all of its dangers and faults, can teach us some pretty valuable lessons about approaching work and life with purpose. If you sit down at the card table with the idea that something will just sort of happen, you will be disappointed.

Here's the part where you wonder if we used the word "purpose" just then but really meant strategy, or perhaps preparation. We didn't. For some, "purpose" is a reference to personal philosophy or spiritual orientation. Which is great. In this conversation, however, it's about creating results for yourself and others. **Purpose is a clear, specific reason for why you are doing (or not doing) a thing.** It is a framework that determines who you would hire and what they would do. It is a clear definition of why a product or service exists. *It is the answer to why.* It is distinct from strategy, tactics, vision, etc. In fact, it is the essential first step to all of those things. Purpose is acknowledging that you came to win at cards, not merely to play, and that you accept the responsibility that comes with it.

The risks of purposelessness are fairly obvious within the confines of a simple game. The rules are universal, and the outcomes are immediate and obvious. Bad play is punished, good play is rewarded, and we can see that individuals who guide their approach from a place of purpose find more success. Those who truly intend to win and then do what it takes to win—learn, practice, hustle, try—tend to win the most.

Move the conversation into the real world of life and work, and things start to seem much more complicated. The rules are unclear, the outcomes hard to define, and everything seems dependent on your point of view. But in reality, most of what we encounter in our professional lives is an endless parade of people who have showed up to the table without a clear idea of who or what they are. They are hoping for good cards. They are waiting for their turn. They lack purpose.

At this point, it would be understandable if many of you feel the urge to disagree. People do have purpose! They want to make money and support their loved ones and create things through their work. All true. The difference we're pointing to is the level of success they allow themselves to aim for. Everyone wants to play, everyone would like to win, but not everyone accepts the responsibility of what it takes *to win*. And not necessarily because they are afraid of hard work. More often than not, it is fear of failure that holds them back.

There is a big difference between committing yourself to being a leader and waiting to see if other people choose you to be their leader. The first holds purpose, the second is fear that requires validation to act. It is the *inferno* that drives us, our teams and our companies every day.

Think of purpose as a kind of career penicillin, a magic cure against some of the worst ailments that afflict individuals and organizations. Purpose prevents the big three: career quagmire, blob-like bureaucracy, and pointless stuff masquerading as valuable products or services. Let's break these down in order.

Career quagmire is the crisis of *just good enough*. It sounds muddy and gooey but in truth, it often looks pretty good from the outside. It's the job you don't love that pays just a little too well to ever leave. It leads to days and weeks that blur together without memorable moments of self-expression or connection with others. What began as a career that enabled your life (be married, buy a house, have two cars, etc.) has become a life that has paralyzed your career—too many obligations, too many people depending on you to ever really consider leaving or doing something different. It's a tough, tough spot in which millions of people find themselves.

A purpose-driven mindset, on the other hand, unlocks the individual as a leader in their life and work, and creates the possibility of real change.

Bureaucratic corporate bloat (we like to call it "the blob") is an indication of an organizational lack of purpose. It is so notoriously difficult to scale and maintain the same energy and vitality of a startup that many people think corporate bloat is inevitable past a certain headcount. Regardless, rudderless companies attract purposeless people—it's much easier for them to look professional and seem like they know what they are doing inside a blob (large corporation)—and the effect is toxic to innovation, agility, morale, and more.

Finally, purposelessness can show up in products or services that lack clear value propositions. Born from endless weekly scheduled meetings and groupthink, these offerings clog the internet with indecipherable taglines, minor variations on what is already available in the marketplace, and endless, reactive updates intended to help it keep up with perceived competition. Individuals and companies that lack (or have lost) purpose make stuff that is exactly that—*stuff*. Stuff that clutters desktops, drawers, and hard drives.

An individual whose purpose is to lead and create does not end up in a career cul-de-sac. That person holds the power to gather others around a vision bigger than themselves and operate together with purpose. This prevents bloat and maintains a lean, flexible infrastructure. Working from purpose instead of a fear of failure, these teams produce radically new products and services that hold clear, compelling reasons for existence. Employees are excited to maintain these products and make them better over time through constant optimization. This sequence involves many other concepts and connections (more on that in other sections), but it is clear that purpose is the spark that lights the fire.

If it isn't obvious already, purpose is simply a decision. It is the courage to choose and act from that choice without any outside permission or invitation. That's why it lights up all of our fears and insecurities—it requires us to commit to something and risk failure. That risk produces energy and that energy fuels everything to follow. The alternative? Hope you draw some good cards, knowing your purpose behind them. Hang around and see if your luck turns.

CHAPTER THREE

Power

Everyone can relate to the experience of being made to do something. It connects to our earliest memories of childhood and the authority of parents. School, summer camp, first job… all important and enriching, and all colored with the feeling of transaction in order to succeed. I do what you say, and you allow me to do or have something. We are raised to believe there is always someone with power over us—either by virtue of sheer size, parental responsibility, disciplinary authority, or just being the person who cuts the paychecks. Behaving (subordinating your own desires to conform with the wishes of the powerful) is what kept your allowance flowing, kept you on the basketball team, or allowed you to study abroad. And all the while, you dreamed of a day when you would be more powerful.

For a lot of people, their conception of power was fully baked right then and there. They've found bigger words and more complicated ways of describing it, but fundamentally, they see power as leverage, a circumstantial force that enables one party to make the other party do (or not do) something. To them, power is granted by position and afforded to those who are lucky enough to inherit it or ruthless enough to seize it for themselves.

In this book, we see power a little differently. Understanding power is critical to unlocking deeper levels of leadership, co-creation, and obviously empowerment (all covered in separate chapters). For the moment, we'll focus on this phenomenon we call power, something many people say when they really mean control or coercion.

Power is unrestricted access to the possibility of change. Self-granted, it has no limit and cannot be taken from you. It is accessible anywhere, at any time, and it moves between people to make things happen. Applied thoughtfully, it acts more like a spark or a current, an electrical reaction that lights up and activates anyone around it. Others can plug into it, discover their own power, and add to the supply. In other words, it is nothing whatsoever like what you experienced from the shift manager at your summer job during high school.

Many of our early experiences with what we thought was power were actually encounters with coercion or bribery. Coercion is influencing someone by the threat of force. Bribery means influencing someone by the promise of a reward. Both tactics can produce action, but neither unlocks the potential of the subject and truly changes the environment.

Our conception of power is inextricably linked to creation and change. Power makes new things happen while coercion and bribery enforce and extend the hierarchy that was already in place. Think about it—most of your negative experiences with what you thought was power were designed to protect the position of the "powerful" and ensure that others remained less powerful. An endless process of pushing others down in order to keep oneself up, it stifles curiosity and creativity, fosters ill will, and creates very, very predictable (and limited) results.

Productive power, change-making power, moves toward goals that are far bigger than any individual and aligns people according to purpose and action. It's not hierarchical and doesn't flow from an interest in personal positioning or political gain. You have undoubtedly experienced power in this form, although you may not have recognized it as such. You may have seen it as "something we're all excited about" or "so and so believes in me" or "this is the opportunity of a lifetime!" These are all interactions with power flowing between people to produce change. It's the opposite of feeling like you've been made to do something and instead is an experience of freedom to act toward an outcome you truly desire.

You can produce power in yourself. You can share it with others to create and change things. And you can cultivate it in any organization.

1) Power production.

Access to personal power begins with training yourself to see everything as a possibility. This can take some time and patience as there is probably a lot to un-learn here. First, consider something relatively simple and small, like decluttering a room in your house, avoiding junk food for a single day, or keeping a positive attitude at work for a week. Listen as the cascade of circumstances and explanations flood your brain, the immediate and automatic self-talk that assures you that the task is impossible. Let it happen, get it all out, and offer up all the reasons why not. Then choose to make one thing different. Ignore the noise and grant yourself the power to be different in one small way.

On a small scale, this is the beginning of individual power production. It is mastery over self-limitations and the realization that you have the power to change anything. As you apply this power, you'll find that instead of running out, your supply has grown. More can change. Previous changes have uncovered new possibilities. And others have begun to notice.

2) Power sharing.

Having accessed some power, you will undoubtedly notice others experiencing you differently. Resist the urge to loudly announce yourself as a powerful person—you are not a super-hero yet—and consider the possibilities of working with others to make something happen. Remember, the power started flowing when you focused on a tangible task. Seeing yourself as a person who can declutter a room produced the power necessary to declutter the room. The same applies as we seek to share power and access what is possible for others. This begins with a careful consideration of where they are coming from and what you could do together that would align with your common interests or goals.

The simplest expression of sharing power is listening to someone else from a place of learning instead of waiting it out so you can get what you want. Ask them what it's like to be them, to work with you, to see the world from their perspective. And then just listen. That's all. Really listen and absorb what they have to say and thank them for the gift of their time and effort. This simple act will have them see you differently and change what they think is possible between you. From there, you can consider acting together and applying your power as a team.

3) Power cultivation.

At an organizational level, cultivation of power requires consistent, purposeful attention. It will wax and wane with differences in individual backgrounds and motivations. All organizations are vulnerable to slipping into coercive habits by virtue of their size—group psychology takes hold and before you know it, politics and hierarchy and leverage become the norm. In order to maintain a healthy supply of creative power, leaders must identify goals beyond the enrichment and/or further empowerment of themselves. They must listen to their teams and hire managers that know how to listen. They must commit to helping their people be better (bureaucracies call this human capital development) through training, counseling, full-spectrum feedback, and other tools for interpersonal enrichment.

Even with all that, you'll find that power is in pretty short supply in large organizations. It happens in bursts or individual efforts, but the idea of holding this definition of power in place throughout a company of more than 150 people is incredibly difficult. More often, companies are founded through powerful, visionary partnerships and small teams and then grow into powerless blobs (large corporations). And that's okay! Corporate blobs pay people, offer health benefits, and sustain the economy. But if you have a personal experience of power, if you really harness it and start to make something amazing happen, I doubt you'll ever be truly happy inside of a corporate blob again. And that's the other thing we should mention about productive power—it's addictive.

Don't say we didn't warn you.

CHAPTER FOUR

Integrity

Is it wrong to be late for a meeting? It's annoying, maybe even infuriating, but is it morally or ethically wrong? Inside the vast majority of businesses, most people would say no; being a little late for a meeting is a minor offence.

Similarly, telling a colleague you will send something on a Thursday and then actually sending it on a Friday isn't only excusable, it's typical. It doesn't take very long in any career to start actively planning for it, assuming that everyone you work with has their own relationship to time and effort and accountability and your mileage may vary. Until or unless unpredictable behavior reaches extreme levels, we accept it as the norm and operate around it within companies of all sizes.

We tend to think of unreliable behavior as unfortunate but unavoidable, and separate it from the purposeful deceit we consider to be morally wrong. In reality, we're just asking the wrong question. Is being late to the meeting wrong? No. Is it unhelpful? Absolutely yes and the damage is much greater than most organizations imagine.

This brings us to the concept of integrity. It's common to hear that term and immediately think of it in moral or ethical terms, as a reference to right or just behavior. While that may be useful in some contexts, we're asking you to think of it in engineering terms: the state of being whole or undivided. The "integrity" of a suspension bridge is a reference to **whether or not it is whole, complete, intact, and ready for the use for which it was designed.** If the bridge is missing some cables (out of integrity), we would not consider it to be morally wrong, we would simply consider it unsafe to cross.

Now back to the delayed meeting, missed deadline, etc. When a person says they will be somewhere or do something, and then fails to be there or to do it, they are out of integrity. They have not kept their word. This doesn't make them a "bad" person, it simply means their colleagues don't know if they can be counted on. The bridge appears a little rickety, so to speak.

As a thought experiment, imagine that you and everyone you work with did exactly what they said they would do exactly when they said they would. In circumstances where anyone was truly prevented from remaining in integrity, they notified all parties of the situation and were accountable for cleaning up whatever mess was caused by it. This is so foreign to the typical professional experience it may take a minute to truly process the implications. What if you knew exactly what you could count on from each member of your team through honest, direct, transparent communication? What if you spent none of your time calculating, revising, theorizing, and accommodating unintegral behavior?

The most obvious benefit of personal and organizational integrity is speed. Not that people necessarily work harder or faster but their work benefits from the clarity of actually knowing what is or isn't going to happen. The less obvious but more important benefit is trust. Integral behavior accelerates trust and in turn, unlocks innovation, collaboration, and more.

To take a closer look at integrity as we've defined it here, let's consider the example of a manager asking a team member for a report by the end of the week. In an environment lacking integrity, the following things are probably going on:

- The manager actually needs it by the end of the week after but expects the team member to turn it in late, so she invents an early deadline. She's experienced him turning things in late and can't trust him with the real deadline.
- The team member knows his manager invents and subsequently forgets deadlines. He doubts his manager will remember the request and carelessly agrees, assuming she will remind him at some point if she really wants it.
- Immediately after ostensibly agreeing to the delivery of a report by the end of the week, neither party truly knows when (if ever) the report will be handed in.

Written out like that, it sounds ridiculous. In reality, this situation occurs all the time, and the inefficiency it produces is mind-blowing. It is two people play-acting the roles of manager and team member to an audience of no one at no benefit to either party or the company at large.

At this point, you might be thinking, *This is simply the way things are.* Humans are imperfect, trust is a rare commodity, $@%$ happens and life goes on. We do the best we can. Right?

Wrong. This is a defeatist viewpoint, and a higher level of integrity really is realistic, attainable, and worth pursuing as a competitive edge. Here's how you get there:

1) Living and leading with integrity begins with keeping one's word to oneself.

    It is impossible to demonstrate and teach integral behavior if you cannot keep a promise to yourself. This doesn't mean you will be perfect but rather that you will be conscious of your personal integrity and committed to what you have set out for yourself. You may be reading this and seeing it as recrimination for never getting up early to run like you tell yourself you will the night before. Quite the opposite. If it doesn't work for you to get up early and run, look yourself in the mirror and declare that you will sleep in until the last possible moment before you have to get ready to go to work. Tell yourself the truth. Once you get in the habit of being honest with yourself, discovering a time to run will get much easier.

2) Start keeping your word with others.

For many, this is simply learning to stop agreeing with every-thing anyone asks you to do. This can feel like setting yourself up to disappoint, but weigh your fear of saying no with how it feels to neglect something you said you would do. The momentary, short-term pain avoidance of thoughtless agreement is usually dwarfed by the real-world anger, awkwardness, and mistrust created by the failure to keep an agreement. Keeping your word doesn't mean you gain the power to bend time and space and are never, ever late again. It simply means the minute you realize you won't be able to keep your word, you reach out to make it known and take responsibility for whatever the impact was on others involved.

3) Finally, and only after truly devoting yourself to Steps 1 and 2, ask for others to keep their word with you and focus on relationships that have integrity as a founding principle.

You'll find that keeping your word to yourself and others will actually produce this for you—people won't want to let you down because you don't let them down. Integral behavior is attractive, and others will be eager to work with you and for you because of the clarity possible through your commitment to integrity.

Over time, integral practices will help you identify business partners and investors, it will change the way you hire and become a cornerstone of any organization you lead. Not because it's the morally right thing to do, but because it works.

CHAPTER FIVE

Performance

A baseball makes a particular sound when struck at an extremely high speed by a wooden bat. If you hear it up close, it literally sounds like a crack—like a giant tree suddenly splitting. The naked eye can't actually track the exact linear trajectory of a 95-mile-per-hour fastball moving from the pitcher's hand to the bat to the seats in right field. It starts out as a blur, explodes with the sound of contact, and slows into consistent view as the ball arcs into the stands. The experience is as much auditory as it is visual. In the modern scientific game of baseball, this is called an outcome.

Heralded by Michael Lewis's seminal book *Moneyball: The Art of Winning an Unfair Game*, the information age eventually found the national pastime, much to the chagrin of many of its players and managers. They complained that computer-generated analysis distorted the game, that an experienced eye was more valuable than a computer. Ultimately, they argued that only someone who has played the game can really evaluate another player. And…

They were wrong. In the years that followed the publication of *Moneyball*, the advantages of so-called sabermetrics (the mathematical and statistical analysis of baseball records) became overwhelming and indisputable, and now every team employs a cadre of data scientists, researchers, and, well, nerds.

The feeling of baseball is much the same as it ever was. The sound of the ball striking the bat defies calculation and is still thrilling to hear in person. And yet the game is very different. Strategies and tactics are very different than they were 30 years ago. Lineups are different, player evaluations are different, and the vernacular (outcome) is unrecognizable from a generation ago. All of this occurred because of an intense desire to win. Baseball teams with limited resources to compete for top players, desperate to find an edge, got serious about finding advantages wherever they could. And they wanted to win so badly—for money, for pride, for prestige, for survival—that they were willing to risk every sacred cow the sport held dear on the altar of improvement. These teams utilized data in new ways to expose the myths of team building and find value in players that richer teams had overlooked. They got smarter. As a result, they won more often.

There's nothing wrong with getting smarter to perform better.

If you want to win, you have to be willing to build a culture of performance.

Performance is purposeful action, aimed at a specific outcome, exposed to analysis to determine its value. This is distinct from artistic performance, a subjective act of expression. We're talking about swing-the-bat performance, actions that produce hits or misses (outcomes) in a way that leads to changes in strategy and tactics to maximize your opportunity to win.

Professional baseball players initially resisted this concept because it disadvantaged them. If a player hit a long home run, that player would prefer that his coach remember that feeling of awe, of watching the ball arc into the stands, instead of thinking about how that player can only hit a home run once every 75 at-bats. The same logic applies to software developers, marketers, engineers, and architects. We would all prefer to be remembered for our best work as opposed to our average impact of our work, over time, adjusted for conditions.

Achieving a culture of performance is difficult. Amazon, a clear leader in data-driven analysis among major corporations, famously outlawed so-called "weasel words" from its internal vocabulary. Instead of using phrases like "nearly all" or "significantly better" in emails and memos, team members were encouraged to cite a specific number without editorial commentary. The thinking being that good or bad, the number can speak for itself. Staffers were also encouraged to respond to questions with one of four Amazon answers: yes, no, a number, or "I don't know" along with a plan to find out.

Has Amazon figured it out? It's difficult to argue with its valuation but also hard to ignore the searing criticism of its former executives and front-line employees. At such a vast scale, performance can easily morph from cultural touchstone to de-humanizing constraint. What we want is an organizational desire for optimization that aligns with our team members' individual goals. So how do we get there? What does it take to instill a performance mindset?

1) Hire people who love the game.
   By and large, baseball players overcame their opposition to next-level performance analysis because they love what they do, and the rewards of doing it well are too great to pass up. Look for innate enthusiasm, a compulsive desire to hone a craft, and a short memory for failure. Big league pitchers know within milliseconds of releasing the ball if they've made a huge mistake (see: crack of the bat). Great pitchers live with the public nature of the result and come back moments later to compete all over again. Their desire to perform, combined with a willingness to do so in an observable and outcomes-driven environment, gives them an excellent opportunity to improve and succeed.

2) Expand available performance time for yourself and everyone around you.
   Consider your own schedule—is it populated with large gaps of time where your desired outcomes aren't clear or trackable? Are

you investing significant amounts of your day in preparation, distraction, recovery, etc.? Look for ways to declutter your day and fill it with blocks of time spent on the field of play. Chop your "administrative" time in half and devote the recovered hours to new client prospecting. You will either succeed or fail (data!). Success means a higher budget and the opportunity to hire an administrative assistant. Failure exposes a problem you would never administrate yourself out of anyways. Examine your team's schedule. Is your developer in meetings all the time? Figure out why everyone is constantly hanging around in the metaphorical dugout and get them back on the field, where they can perform, be observed, and succeed in measurable terms.

3) Brace yourself to accept the results of performance analysis, whatever they are.

The performers on your team don't always look or act like you would expect them to. They are, in fact, the people who will move your ideas forward and create value for you and everyone you hope to reach through your company. Be prepared to deal with your own bias and accept the data for what it is. In the long run, building a culture of performance will be far more satisfying than a culture of compatible personalities, similar worldviews, or simply collecting people you like.

Distilled down to its essence, performance is nothing more than a willingness to allow someone to watch what you do. That observation (analysis) produces insights and opportunities for improvement. The pain of watching your last pitch sail over your head toward the bleachers is the fuel that drives you to improve your technique so get on the field along with everyone else on your team and learn to love the game.

CHAPTER SIX

Objectivity

We have no opinions whatsoever about herbal tea. We're not tea drinkers, never have been, and couldn't tell you the first thing about the various blends or varieties or whatever they're called. We would prefer that tea leaves were harvested sustainably; we'd like for everyone who works in the industry to earn a fair wage for their labor, and we hope that it is processed and packaged in a way that makes it completely safe to consume. But we don't think about herbal tea on a regular basis.

Our indifference for tea makes it easy to achieve near-perfect objectivity on the subject. Because we don't care, it's easy to see it for what it is and judge any variety of it (or company that sells it) based solely on its performance. If you love tea, you may think we're missing out, but you can't argue with the clarity that our indifference produces. It's easy to see this in your own life as well—consider a harmless and uninteresting product or service, one that you are neither for nor against, and you'll quickly discover your own clear-eyed view of it. Now ponder your most closely held interests and passions, and you'll find the opposite.

Almost everyone seeks to work in industries that interest or inspire them. Most founders and funders are drawn to ventures that they actually care about. They have a point of view on the matter at hand. And while this point of view fuels passion and creates energy to produce or promote something, it brings a few other characteristics to the party as well. As soon as we identify something as being important to us, we open ourselves up to the possibility of rejection by those who see it differently. This is a critical distinction.

One of the most prevalent and persistent ways individuals express their worldview and protect themselves from rejection is through judgment. For us, deciding between soup or salad at lunch is simply a choice. Believing that salad is the only possible valid choice and that anyone who chooses soup is wrong is judgment. Expressions of judgment are rooted in the premise that "my truth is *the* truth" and that truth is equally valid and true for others as well. **Objectivity, or non-judgment, is bringing yourself to something with the idea that it can only be measured based on what it does or produces, not whether or not it aligns with my particular worldview.** If you like soup, order the soup; if you don't, don't. Either one is fine so long as it produces a successful lunch.

Back to herbal tea for a moment. You probably noticed that there are a few things we do hold opinions about (sustainability, equity of opportunity, safety), even when it comes to tea. These are considerations that we believe *make the world work better*. You may disagree and your disagreement does not mean we wish any misfortune on you in this world or the next. We point back to it as a means to clarify objectivity as we're using it here. We're not talking about sociopathic amorality that would justify murdering your competition to gain a competitive edge. What we mean is working toward and calling others to the highest possible level of objectivity within the work or project you've set out to accomplish together.

Once you train yourself to become more aware of it, you'll find judgment and its toxic effects all over the workplace. Individuals who self-identify as hard workers hold judgment for those who do not appear to put the same effort in. Investors judge founders for expenditures that they consider to be unnecessary. Apple loyalists judge PC diehards, and so on. In every instance, one party's need to be right—to see them themselves as living correctly—impedes their ability to work with another party. Judgment is very, very difficult to conceal and often presents itself as contempt. We've all seen someone look at us and seem to be thinking: *How could you possibly behave this way? How could you think something so wrong?*

In reality, everyone simply works and thinks differently. The presumably lazy colleague might be the genius that solves the glitch in your software platform. The fiscally irresponsible startup founders might indeed be fiscally irresponsible and still make their investor a fortune. The Apple and PC people probably just have different technology needs. In every instance, if the judgmental party was solely committed to the success of the company or the collaboration, the judgment would instantly be replaced with some form of measurement. And the measurement would determine whether a colleague needs to put in more hours, whether the founders should spend less, or if we should force everyone to use MacBooks. Instead, these individuals hold a conflicting commitment—to being right—in addition to their relationship to the company.

Identifying and managing the urge to be right takes time and practice. Moreover, this phenomenon looks very different depending on where the individual sits within the power dynamic of a relationship or company. It is relatively easy for a founder with sole ownership of the company to declare that the best idea will win, even if it isn't hers. She will undoubtedly benefit from the idea and, for her, this is merely an act of controlling the ego. For anxious team members who may be worried about job security or career prospects, an additional incentive is present to appear "right" and carefully avoid the appearance of ever being "wrong".

From here, we can see that there are multiple layers to the challenge for anyone looking to make a big dent in the world. First, they must consider their own relationship to judgment and strive for higher levels of objectivity in everything they do. A simple way to find progress on this is to continually ask yourself why you want something to be a certain way. Is it really and truly the best possible way to do it? Can you demonstrate it so that others can see your way is verifiably superior, or is it simply the way you want it done? If your aim is to be effective—as opposed to being "right"—you'll find many opportunities for improvement with little difficulty.

As you engage with others to found companies and projects, intentionally create them as non-judgmental environments. This means speaking plainly and directly about the concept of objectivity within the culture you aim to create and acting in demonstration of it. Having partners and team members see you apply objectivity will be exciting for them, as it produces true meritocracy. The individuals and ideas that work best in service to the aim of whatever you are doing will be rewarded appropriately. Underperforming individuals will be clear that conditions of their employment (or termination) have no relationship to subjective belief systems or discriminatory practices.

Finally, it is essential to balance practical objectivity with big-picture moral and ethical considerations. It is entirely possible to be perfectly objective about the performance of your herbal tea company while taking an uncompromising stance on health or safety. This is where explicitly declaring your value set enables teams, investors, and customers to choose whether or not they wish to align themselves with it. If environmental sustainability (your truth) is more important to you than profits, ensure that all stakeholders know this and can take it into account before committing themselves to you. From there, you could see a company that only purchases Fairtrade tea leaves COULD ALSO launch an apple spice flavor that the founder absolutely loathes but will be meaningful to their success as a company.

The impulse to judge and hold your own viewpoint as correct is hard-wired into all of us. Rather than fighting this urge, or pretending it doesn't exist, create a discussion around this for yourself and your collaborators in order to strive for higher and higher levels of objectivity.

Over coffee, preferably.

CHAPTER SEVEN

Destination

Most adults have experienced the phenomenon of driving somewhere without any conscious recollection of the roads that took us there. It's so common, in fact, it's unremarkable. When we've grown accustomed to the route, we rely on muscle memory and reflex to keep us on the road, and the mind wanders. This so-called "inattentional blindness" is simply your brain being economical with scarce resources. Operating on autopilot frees it up to do other things.

New destinations, on the other hand, require attention. They require GPS, two hands on the wheel, and your passenger to pipe down during tricky highway merges. Finding new places makes it harder to internally multitask, and demands an outward-looking expression of concentration and awareness.

The familiarity of your commute, on the other hand, allows for a couple of things. For many, it opens up a space for the passive intake of information through radio, podcasts, etc. For others, it serves as unstructured thinking time where they can worry, reconsider past decisions, obsess over the possibilities of the day, etc. Neither of these activities are wrong, per se, but neither are they particularly productive. And we would submit that most of you reading this right now spend far more time alternating between these two states of being than you would like to admit, far more than would fit inside your commute. These two states—

distracted or anxious—can fill a day, a week, or even a career. But going somewhere you've never been before limits your capacity for these activities. It demands that your attention and focus remain outward, conscious of the world around you and tracking your progress toward an established goal.

The distraction/self-obsession dichotomy plagues individuals and teams. It is the natural resting state for countless people. Depending on your philosophical worldview, consciousness is a blessing or a curse. Either way, the primary means of dealing with it is to distract oneself from it by becoming the passive recipient of information inputs or to sit and stew about the process of being alive. Destination is a critical component of moving past these states into something productive and meaningful. This mindset can reshape a career, unify a team, and create results.

Conventional motivational teaching is goal-oriented and transactional. It posits that you are more likely to achieve a given outcome if you clearly define it and set yourself toward it with purpose. This is true! But it's not what we mean when we talk about creating a destination or moving with a destination mindset. In this concept, we want to focus on what the act of navigating toward a destination produces in you. The you that is *going somewhere* is different to the one that is simply *being somewhere.* Unfortunately, the lure of just being in stasis, conserving energy, enjoying distraction, and scratching your self-involved psychological itches is very, very powerful.

Destination is a willingness to commit to a defined, external outcome in order to access the version of yourself that appears when you move toward it. In considering this definition, it's important to note that arriving at any single destination will never, ever be "enough". There will never be enough money or fame or validation to change who you are. You will still be you. A seven-digit exit from your successful startup will almost certainly breed the desire to do it again. Earning a patent on your mind-blowing invention will inspire you to tinker with your next invention. For us, destination is goal-oriented energy maintained over time, with no individual goal as the endpoint or the termination of effort. So, in this context, destination is distinct from goals in that we see destination as a way of thinking and a goal as a signpost along the way.

While a few of us are truly and positively destination-oriented and from an early age have enjoyed the experience of being in motion toward achievement, many are not. Some discover destination through tragedy or failure—marked by experience, they work maniacally to never experience it again. Most are socialized to pretend to have goals in order to fit into an achievement-oriented culture. In reality, these individuals are motivated by relationships and fear of failure. Having access to people they care about and avoiding negative consequences creates their goals for them.

There is nothing bad about valuing relationships or avoiding negative consequences but there is something incredible about learning to develop a destination mindset in addition to everything else you already are. Regardless of where we started out from, most of us have some work to do in rewiring our brains to move toward a destination mindset. To do this, practice these three habits:

1) Notice who and how you are when you are moving with purpose toward a goal.

    This is not the same as tracking progress but rather noting how you felt and what you noticed around you as you moved toward something tangible. For example, let's say you've set out to learn a song on the piano. How did it feel to begin this process? What was set aside to make time to do it? What did it feel like after spending time in practice? You'll likely notice that it felt good to operate with initiative, the time would otherwise have been spent in an anxiety/distraction loop and that having done so motivated you to get something else done unrelated to the piano. Take note! Acknowledge this to yourself and others. Observation and affirmation are key to rewiring the brain so make the process more "real" by reporting on it.

2) Without judgment or criticism, start a list of areas of your life and career that lack destination.

If this exercise becomes self-critical, set it aside and revisit when you can be patient with yourself and others. Look for situations where you are on autopilot or avoiding initiative and simply note them for the record. You can't charge forward in every direction all at once, but you can identify the difference between planned inactivity and inertia. For example, let's say your opportunity for advancement in your career would benefit if you were fluent in Spanish. Setting that as a destination for next year while you apply yourself to other meaningful priorities this year is fine and represents a destination mindset. On the other hand, knowing that you should learn Spanish and not knowing why you haven't started is entirely different and belongs on this list.

3) Challenge yourself and others to be clear and specific about what you are setting out to do.

One of the most challenging aspects of introducing destination-oriented behavior into your life is the distracting effects others can have on you. Teams, departments, and entire organizations fall victim to squishy language that help them avoid accountability. This can be counteracted by simple clarifying questions that convert something from a discussion item to a decision item. An oft-overlooked part of establishing a reputation as someone who gets things done is defining what you are doing in a way that others can notice when it is accomplished. This language serves very small goals just the same as big ones, and introducing it into day-to-day work priorities can make the big goals seem more attainable.

Destination is closely related to leadership, power, co-creation, and other chapters in this book. Accessing those concepts will accelerate any individual or team toward a destination and resolve many of the obstacles along the way. What is important to re-emphasize here is that destination is primarily concerned with *who you become on your way toward it*. That version of you is the one that produces results and helps you find greater satisfaction in what you do.

CHAPTER EIGHT

Focus

Ask anyone what they do for a living and they are likely to reply with a primary function—fundraiser, lawyer, accountant, etc. Ask them to walk you through their day, step-by-step, and notice how much time is actually spent fundraising, litigating or calculating. For many of us, our "work" is increasingly crowded with correspondence, facilitation, administration, and plain old attendance. That's why so many people say they come into the office early just to be able to "get things done".

Most companies are incredibly inefficient due to activity clutter. This is especially true in large corporations (blobs), where individuals are actually incentivized to act busy in the hopes of seeming important (or at least necessary). But the phenomenon persists down to smaller ventures and even startups. This is due in part to the impulse to "play business", acting out the officiousness one associates with a successful company because it looks and feels good. Up to a point this is harmless; excitedly picking out office decor after three years of toiling away in a garage can be a useful release. Taken too far, it becomes a cover for incompetence—a clear indication that a company lacks direction—or simply group hallucination.

Combating busy-ness to create a culture of performance requires focus. **Focus is a habitual state of maximum productivity through careful stewardship of time and energy.**

Getting serious about focus requires a capacity to consider how you and your team operate and whether you are willing to make extreme adjustments in service of productivity. And we do mean extreme. One of the most significant obstacles to achieving a high level of organizational focus is that it brings individuals out of the mainstream of work culture and can foster a fear of seeming weird. When it is normal to waste time and has been normalized for everyone you know going all the way back to kindergarten, optimizing time can look very, very different.

For those willing to achieve higher levels of focus, it begins with the understanding that intensity plays a critical role in productivity. This means that when we are truly ready to do something and have the opportunity to do it, and only it, without distraction, the intensity of our effort increases exponentially. The task is completed faster and at a higher level of quality than would have been possible in a distracted, low-intensity state. This principle runs counter to nearly every major technological and cultural advancement of the modern era.

Most professionals are surrounded by devices invented to keep them in constant communication, working in spaces designed for maximum freedom and visibility, and answering to people who actually believe that multitasking is real and possible. As a result, most professionals operate in a habitual state of low intensity produced by constant distraction and interruption. Worse yet, this state of affairs has re-wired their brains to crave distraction and compulsively seek it out.

Research has demonstrated over and over again that people only do one thing at a time. We simply possess the ability to switch between tasks very quickly, creating the illusion of multitasking. In reality, we are simply doing a few things slowly and at a collective decrease in quality, operating against the way our brains are designed to operate. In his book *Deep Work: Rules for Focused Success in a Distracted World*, Cal Newport distilled the intensity factor into a formula: High-Quality Work Produced = (Time Spent) x (Intensity of Focus). To put it another way, when you maximize intensity while you work, you maximize results produced per unit of time spent working.

How do the highest performers achieve maximum intensity? Phones off, email autoresponders on, physically isolated from colleagues for hours or even days at a time. In other words, the opposite of the modern office environment. However, this level of productivity tunneling is only possible when someone is perfectly prepared to engage in an individual act of productivity. For many of us, our work is necessarily collaborative and truly benefits from some interaction, access, and physical gathering. So, what do we do? Here are three keys to elevating the focus of your team without completely sacrificing the collaborative experience of teamwork:

1) Prioritize tasks.

    Clearly affirming what should be done next, at the expense of everything else if necessary, is essential. This is a little foreign to some groups and as a start, it can be useful to survey the individuals on your team (separately) to understand their existing prioritization models. Every person has one, whether they consciously describe it as such, and it can be extremely revealing to see how it guides their behavior. A lack of clear prioritization leads to base-covering, an attention-spreading exercise designed to "show movement" on multiple fronts. This is both counterproductive and misleading. The other common finding from prioritization surveys is the prevailing sense that simply being available is the most important thing anyone can do. Behaviors like checking email compulsively, answering every phone call, and dropping the task-at-hand for an unplanned meeting are considered virtues in most workplaces. Eliminate the availability myth and empower your team to block large chunks of time for deep concentration.

2) Batch similar activities.

While we may only be able to focus on one thing at a time, collecting similar things within defined periods allows us to minimize so-called "attention residue" that builds up when we force the brain to shift gears between entirely different tasks. The notion of aggregating calls or meetings into one day and writing tasks into another isn't necessarily new. In fact, many professionals have attempted it and would have you know that they couldn't make it work. This is why organizational adoption of batching practices is so critical. Having one team member declare Tuesdays to be "meeting day," and the rest of the team scheduling meetings five days of the week is obviously unworkable. Which brings us back to the fear of seeming weird. Startups and small ventures that have succeeded in batching activities have done so by moving individual productivity days out of the office, by reassigning people to new roles to better balance task pacing, and even by "closing" altogether (everyone's email sends an out-of-office response) for days dedicated to internal activity. The key here is the willingness to actually do it.

3) Regularly isolate.

The joy of making something happen is in the journey, not the payoff. That joy is closely connected to the camaraderie of the team and the experience of doing something together. The attraction of being in the office is powerful, particularly when so many have had an extended, enforced period of pandemic isolation already. But if you are committed to performance and interested in gaining the benefit of focus, it is almost impossible to imagine a scenario where everyone on your team should be in the office together every day. It's simply too costly. But rather than simply declare that people can take remote days whenever they want, walk everyone through the concept of focus and plan with them to identify clear goals to be achieved while away from distractions. The point of isolation is maximum intensity and that requires an extremely low level of distraction. If a home environment can't deliver what is needed, find a space where people can go that liberates them from the distractions of both team and family.

Achieving higher levels of focus offers an added benefit to the obvious upside in productivity. The more time you spend focused on making something amazing, the less time you spend obsessing over your competition, worrying about what other people think, or generally getting lost in pointless distraction/anxiety loops. Each and every day offers the same choice—you can be busy or you can be productive.

The choice is yours.

Concepts you work on with someone else

We believe that you need help to do anything of real significance. Most of the joy in doing something comes from the folks you do it with. We're inspired by our colleagues and show up every day to see them and be worthy of their trust. At the same time, people will be the hardest part of whatever you set out to do. Earning their trust, understanding their behavior, aligning yourself with them, and learning what they have to teach can be hard. The best part of everything is also the worst: it's the people.

We're in awe of what is possible when two people commit themselves to acting together. Just two. That nucleus can grow into amazing things, all powered by the bond between one person and another.

The concepts that follow are intended for application between individuals. They are person-to-person tools that can be understood and applied together. Taking each concept seriously, and sincerely engaging in it with another person, will lead to new levels of vulnerability, trust, and possibility for collaboration.

CHAPTER NINE

Co-creation

One of the biggest obstacles to improvisational comedy is learning how to completely trust your fellow performers. To a beginner, improv seems daunting: What if I can't think of anything to say? What if I don't know what to do next? What if the audience hates us? Experienced improv actors know that the solution to these fears is to trust your scene partners.

Bringing yourself on stage with an intention to serve the scene and set your fellow performers up for success unlocks incredible moments of unscripted, unplanned hilarity. But the unpredictable nature of the form is actually rooted in an ironclad commitment: Every great improv performer knows *exactly* what they will do when they take the stage. They will listen, they will accept, and they will expand on their scene partner's premises. They will act from what the scene brings to them. Every time.

All of life is improvised—whether or not it is a comedy is up to you—but the unplanned, unprepared nature of it is rarely more obvious than in the act of entrepreneurship. It is, by definition, doing something you have never done before and doing it in public, where its success or failure will be known and recorded.

More often than not, founders have partners who take the stage with them. A recent MIT survey[1] found that more than

---

[1] https://mitsloan.mit.edu/ideas-made-to-matter/2-founders-are-not-always-better-1

70 percent of startups have two or more founders but the survey also discovered that solo founders were 54 percent less likely to dissolve or suspend their businesses. This is by no means a recommendation from us to start a business by yourself, nor do we see it as clear evidence that going solo is inherently superior; many other factors are involved. It is, however, clear evidence that co-founders *break up all the time*. Clearly, few entrepreneurs understand how to work with each other.

Which brings us back to improv. Why is trust such an obstacle? Because every performer desperately wants to be funny, to get laughs and get noticed and feel the rush of excitement that brought them on stage in the first place. It's not that improv performers fear their scene partners will attack them, there is no danger of actual harm, it's that they fear being left out or marginalized. They fear that someone else will be funnier. Left unchecked, this impulse can create an environment of competition, with performers stepping on each other's lines, mangling the premise, and getting noisier and noisier to no particular purpose.

This is a significant issue for motivated, leadership-minded professionals who have set out to make a dent in the world. As inherently social creatures, the majority of startup founders connect with like-minded collaborators and found companies as teams. This is smart for a million reasons, the most obvious being that the sheer demands of bringing a product or service to life are better served by two (or more) people than one. And then, unfortunately for many startups, things get complicated between the founders and issues arise. Which brings us to the concept of co-creation.

Co-creation is distinct from leadership, empowerment, and other concepts in that it specifically addresses the necessary mindset for two or more people to accomplish something together. Not one person leading the other, or motivating the other, or following the other, rather people acting in unison in service of a purpose larger than any one of them. And it is distinct from collaboration in its declaration of creation— bringing something new into the world as opposed to managing or maintaining whatever already exists.

[Note: if you are reading this and find yourself tuning out because you have no intention of founding a company, take a moment to consider the implications of this concept in other facets of your life. We're using entrepreneurship as a model to explore co-creation, but it is by no means the only arena in which it finds application. This could just as easily be an exploration of why bands break up, marriages fail, project teams underperform, etc. Hang with it and you may find it very relevant to whatever you are up to.]

From this definition—acting together to make something new—we're focusing on what an individual would need to consider about themselves in order for co-creation to even be possible. This is about getting your head in the right place *before you even get on stage* and then being a demonstration of the concept. This is how you get others to see and understand it. Reading through this chapter with the attitude of "wow, this is exactly what my business partner is getting wrong" is a clear signal that there is more work for you to do.

The first step to accessing the ability to co-create is reaching some level of clarity about what you want. It is absolutely true that some people who take improv classes fully intend to become standup comedians. Within themselves, they feel a powerful drive to own their relationship to the audience completely and entertain from a singular, unique viewpoint. There is nothing wrong with that, and it doesn't mean they will necessarily be lousy scene partners. It would, however, be extremely useful for them to recognize that in themselves and be accountable for its implications. Looking for opportunities to sneak in jokes from your standup act during an improv show is improvisational malpractice and absolutely ruins the performance.

Many young entrepreneurs don't know exactly what they want from their careers, and that's okay. That uncertainty can and should be declared and understood by all parties that have committed to each other to start a business. What is critical, particularly for early career founders, is to define their commitment to the venture at hand and make sure they have the flexibility to exit later without destroying the business. The very first principle of performing with others, whether on stage or in an office, must be a commitment to serving the audience. For an improv performer, that means a singular focus on getting laughs, even if they aren't *your* laughs. The show itself must be funny and everything else will take care of itself. In like manner, the business must serve its customers and fulfill on its fundamental premise—to convert your collective ideas and energy into capital.

The second step is building a deep and committed way of listening. Great improv performers listen to their scene partners, listen to their audience, and operate from a place of learning in real time. It is absolutely impossible to listen if you are preoccupied with what you will say or do next. Access to listening only comes with trust. If I don't trust you to involve me in service of our larger aim, I'm likely to shift my attention to what I will do or say irrespective of what you are doing.

Real listening requires being in an active state of not assuming what someone else will say or believing that you already know the answer. It requires a willingness to learn. This can be challenging with anyone, but never more so than when you are in conversation with someone you think you know very well or have worked with for a significant amount of time. We've encountered founding teams through consulting or investing who didn't appear to hear each other at all. Their lack of trust in each other and their assumptions about what the other was thinking led to actual, out loud contradictions they didn't even notice. They had tuned each other out to the point where they could no longer coherently conduct a meeting together.

The third and final step in preparation for co-creation is reserving time and energy to work on the relationship. The vast majority of founding partnerships devote 99 percent of their time on the venture and one percent on their relationship to each other. This is understandable: time is precious and the benefits of "non-essential" interaction between co-founders are harder to quantify than shipping features or billing customers. Unfortunately, fractured relationships end up sinking the venture, oftentimes without much of an effort to repair them.

Making time and effort to maintain healthy co-founder relationships looks like being together away from the venture to understand each other as whole and complete individuals. It means committing to clear, consistent language that helps you navigate disagreements. It means revisiting points of tension over and over with the knowledge that it really might take 50 or more hours of conversation to resolve it. Is that an impossible responsibility when you'll spend literally thousands of hours on the product? Finally, many successful cofounder teams found their way with the aid of a coach or consultant who could help them see themselves more objectively. Don't hesitate to seek help to moderate and facilitate the dialogue between co-founders.

Your business, like any improv show, is entirely made up and no one knows how it will end. To make it successful, your preparation and commitment should be anything but random. So, get clear on what you want, listen and learn from your co-founders, and make time to manage your relationships with them.

It's worth the effort. After all, the audience is out there waiting for you.

CHAPTER TEN

Joy

Neither of us is particularly interested in small talk and we both find ways to skip past some of the more mundane rituals of polite conversation. One way to get to know someone a little faster and find something of actual value to discuss is to subtly dial up the intensity of the terminology you use. For example, the next time someone tells you what they do for a living, ask them if they love it. Most people are not accustomed to this. They may tell you they "like" it or are "fine with" it, but they'll probably hesitate before committing to "love." Unfortunately, most people don't love what they do.

By informally surveying hundreds of people this way over the years, it has become abundantly clear that loving what you do has almost no correlation with compensation. It doesn't correspond with a fancy job title, and surviving medical or law school to become a titled expert doesn't produce love either. These jobs might bring money, safety, security, respect, or some other desirable attribute, but not necessarily joy. Very, very few of us intrinsically enjoy every aspect of what we do, yet some find immense joy in the experience of their work and in the results it produces. One theory holds that some people are just more joyful than others; others claim that anything you have to be paid to do is (by definition) an admission that you don't really enjoy it.

We believe that joy can be consciously created in the context of work and that work itself can be internally redefined into something much deeper than "what I do because I have to." **A joyful mindset is a choice that can be acted upon and supported.** For a deeper exploration on the origination of human happiness and how to access it, we would point you to hundreds of other books from coaches, gurus, and clinical psychologists. For now, we'll continue with the premise that happiness is a choice and discuss the conditions by which you can increase your own and your team's opportunity for joy in your profession.

This process begins with an examination of who you are and why you are doing this job, founding this startup or embarking on this project. You must consciously do it and create dialogue about it within yourself and out loud to anyone with whom you choose to work. Through this dialogue, you can discover your own (and others') trajectory—where they see themselves in the progression of what they have set out to become. Within a team environment, this unlocks recognition and affirmation around a person's intentions, not merely their function or title. Understanding and validating the difference between what someone does and who they have set out to be is a critical component in creating access to joy for them.

Organizations that overlook this step can quickly fall victim to assumptions about why an individual does what they do. Managers and colleagues begin to act and interact from those assumptions, and the individual becomes socialized to meet expectations around a distorted view of themselves. Before too long, an alter ego is created—the version of you at work—that doesn't align with how you see yourself outside of work or how you would want others to see you. It is impossible to experience joy in your work when this occurs.

Having established a way of talking about this challenge and making an effort to connect with people to avoid the creation of alter egos, it is essential to create a culture of acknowledgment.

Notice we're using acknowledgment here, not affirmation, although there is nothing wrong with affirming someone. What we wouldn't want is some sort of automatic affirmation machine, a manager or collective mindset that constantly congratulates everyone for attendance, baseline activities, or birthdays. That kind of mindless recognition can actually reinforce negative habits and pessimistic thinking.

An acknowledgment culture, as we would recommend it, looks like conscious recognition of specific actions that contribute to collective success. An example of this would be crediting a team member for their idea when others use it in a presentation. Sharing positive feedback from a client with an explanation of how a team member's individual actions were connected to the rave review. Noticing and acknowledging when someone goes the extra mile to meet a team deadline when a colleague is on leave. Taken together, these moments foster a positive feedback loop that over time can become embedded in culture. They foster an environment in which each individual feels seen, in which an effort is made to understand them and their contributions are recognized, and which is a place where joy can exist.

Finally, it is essential to tangibly connect your team to the success you've earned together. That's a fancy way of saying "pay them". We'd love to tell you it's all about dialogue and mindfulness, but compensation is the lock that closes and sustains the positivity loop. So, so many leaders and founders struggle with this, face mounting negativity and begin to resent their teams. From the founder's perspective, they were the ones who accepted all the risk, suffered through all the sleepless nights, and created all these jobs in the first place. It's an entirely valid viewpoint, but unfortunately, it always leads to a dead end. Two critical points on compensation that most leaders miss:

1) You don't pay your team to make them happy.

   As noted previously, higher wages don't actually produce joy (or loyalty, or dedication, etc.). You pay them as a concrete form of acknowledgment that validates the bond you've created with them through your work. Unhappiness as a consequence of low compensation is all about feeling neglected or underappreciated, it's not (or rarely) about affording a new car. The money is simply a means of connecting with someone's self-worth and validating the trust they have placed in you.

2) You chose the risk and the sleepless nights and everything that came with starting a business.

   If you intend to grow it to any meaningful size, carrying your feelings about all that into your compensation plan will ensure you stay small. The irony of under-compensation is that it actually sustains the experience of risk, uncertainty, and maximum pressure on the founder. Team turnover increases, culture deteriorates, time is wasted on entrance and exit interviews and for what? So you can prove a point about who got here first? Focus on making your business huge and successful instead of constantly pointing back to what it took to get it underway.

If you've read this far, it's likely that you have some ambition and intention in your life. More than likely you want to create, or already have created, something bigger than yourself. And while there may have been some motivation for you around what you would get out of it, our hope is that this conversation can open up a deeper appreciation for what it's all about. The sooner you realize that the joy is in the journey, the better. Having seen and acknowledged that to yourself, it will be much, much easier to let others in on your joy and create an infectious culture where people can honestly say they love what they do.

CHAPTER ELEVEN

Story

Have you ever wondered why you get songs stuck in your head? Almost all humans struggle with a phenomenon known as "earworms"—sequences of sound and/or rhythm that recur in our brains despite our best efforts to forget them. Unfortunately, they most often seem to be the simplest tunes, like the chorus from a Top 40 hit or the singalong from your kids' animated show. By the time you feel it happening, it's already too late—you'll be humming all day, much to the chagrin of your friends and colleagues.

Earworms seem like a glitch. Some would assume that they occur simply as a process of repetition—if you hear something too many times, it is somehow embedded in your psyche. In reality, sociologists and anthropologists have theorized that earworms likely originate from ways humans communicated tens of thousands of years ago. In pre-literate societies, it was imperative to pass along information for the safety and success of the tribe. This was obviously a verbal exercise and one committed to memory. It is entirely plausible that early societies used rhyme and rhythm to make pieces of information more memorable, such as the location of fresh water, which mushrooms are poisonous, and tribal history and relationships.

This information was important, and in some cases literally meant the difference between life or death so the brain evolved to cling to this information, repeating it internally and memorizing it beyond a shadow of a doubt. The theory goes that certain songs and phrases reawaken this mental muscle, engaging the pre-historical version of ourselves still buried inside our brains. Misperceiving the tune of "Baby Shark" as vital information, the brain repeats it ad nauseam.

The point about earworms is that humans are built to retain information through structured communication that most often takes the shape of a story. A song is, if nothing else, a story set to words. Stories are how we as a species have made sense out of the world since the dawn of time. And somehow, just a few millennia later, we forget this when we create partnerships and businesses and products.

Story is the fundamental tool by which your intentions find connection in others. If you've set out to create a business and make a difference in the world, that business is itself a story. Your path to creating it is a story. And your product or service have stories as well, ideally stories that connect to the emotion and intention of your audience.

FreshBooks is a small business accounting platform. It is literally a pile of code on a server that performs functions but it has a story. The FreshBooks story begins back in January 2003, when Mike was running a four-person design agency. When it came to billing clients, Word and Excel were frustrating to use and weren't built to create professional-looking invoices. Then one day something happened that makes every small business owner cringe: he accidentally saved over an old invoice. Knowing there had to be a better way, Mike decided to create it himself. Over the next two weeks, he coded up a solution that became the foundation of what is now FreshBooks.

Contrast the FreshBooks story with this description from Oracle's NetSuite:

NetSuite SuiteSuccess Starter Edition is a total solution designed to help small and rapidly growing companies manage all aspects of their business in a single system. Packaging the experience gained from tens of thousands of deployments worldwide amassed over two decades into a set of leading practices, NetSuite SuiteSuccess Starter Edition will have you up and running quickly with pre-configured KPIs, workflows, reminders, reports and value-driven dashboards for daily and strategic needs—for all key roles within your business from day one.

No disrespect to the fine folks at Oracle, but can you see the difference? Story moves and motivates through relatability. In the FreshBooks example, we're introduced to a protagonist who experiences a challenge we can relate to. He confronts the challenge and overcomes it through innovation. This is, in essence, the story of being human. The NetSuite description lacks a pulse. It is a non-human voice from the void, rambling about something that doesn't appear to connect in any way to what it feels like to be a person.

Understanding the power of story is critical in building out an organization and having your audience understand and act in response to whatever you have to offer. It should be consciously created, repeated frequently, and baked into everything you share. The basic elements of the story are as follows:

1) A person (or persons) with an intention.

   Every story is about people. Every single one. The only thing that really matters to anyone is other people and the process of understanding themselves and others through communication between people. Yes, non-human elements play a significant role in storytelling, but what actually matters is a person at the center of it (the subject we see ourselves through) and their efforts to connect with others. *The Shawshank Redemption* isn't about prison, it's about the enduring power of friendship. *The Godfather* isn't about crime, it's about family. *Romeo and Juliet* isn't about politics, it's about love. All these stories begin with a person with an intention. In the case of the FreshBooks origin story, we have Mike and his desire to run a successful agency.

2) An obstacle.

   Humans have an innate desire to rearrange the world around them, to make it different in order to bring us closer to others or whatever we desire. Unlike trees, which simply survive wherever they happen to grow and eventually die in the same spot, all humans navigate the terrain around them, literally and metaphorically. We experience literal obstacles, such as mountains or rivers, and figurative obstacles, such as an obstinate cofounder or unsolved technical dilemma. The nature of story is to reveal the human in association with the challenge. This is inherently interesting to us because we can learn from it and discover something about ourselves in the process. It's why you never see movies in which everything goes well and everyone gets along. Heroes need an obstacle, and stories require a challenge at the center. For poor Mike, we learn that he saved over an old invoice. His invoicing process had broken down. He needed to invoice his clients in order to earn revenue and succeed in his intention (run a successful agency). What will he do?

3) A resolution.

For Mike, for Andy Dufresne, even for Michael Corleone (*Shawshank Redemption/Godfather* protagonists), we want to know what happens next. We are anxious to learn whether or not our hero won or lost. Did Andy get away from Shawshank? Will Michael sell his soul to save his family? Did Mike ever send another invoice? Good stories offer their audiences a way through the crisis so they can see what came of it and apply it to their own experience. Note that stories do not necessarily need happy endings; a failure can be every bit as dramatic and instructive as a success. Either way, the story must pay off with a resolution.

Startup founders usually get very good at telling their stories to each other and to their funders and early adopters. These stories usually circulate via transaction (justification for investment) or osmosis (we work around the clock together and sooner or later the story is told). Where the process breaks down is company scale, when new hires don't have close proximity to founders and the original impetus for storytelling has shifted to suit end users and customers.

This narrative gap—the area where a company seems to simply exist, absent the clear definition of hero or challenge or resolution—is where lifeless corporate language starts to take root. Worse than useless, this problem actually clouds the original story itself, confusing teams and partners and leaving stakeholders with conflicting and competing versions of the truth.

Everyone that works for you and with you should have a clear, compelling story as to why the venture exists. That story should inform the stories of specific products and services, the story of the team, the office, so on and so forth. All humans are natural storytellers and we all seek story to make sense out of our lives. If you don't proactively share the story of your company, the members of your company will invent their own so seize the opportunity to tell an honest, authentic, inspiring story that will be *the* story of whatever you are doing.

If you do it well enough, it just might get stuck in your colleagues' and customers' heads.

CHAPTER TWELVE

Design

This book was designed by someone. So were the shoes on your feet, the car you drove today, and the chair you will sit on to eat your next meal. The relative success of the design and how it enhances the experience of whatever you are doing is up to you. Nevertheless, someone has thought long and hard about the experience of the book you are reading, the shoes you are wearing, the car you drove, and the chair you're sitting in and has made choices that define what each object has become in its real and constructed state.

Design is everywhere, and the concept of design is closely linked to commitment and conscious creation. Making something is, if nothing else, the final decision on what you *won't* make. To put it another way, I can think about furniture, I can ponder tables and chairs, I can consider carpentry and joinery, and I can ruminate on all the possibilities that could become a useful object in my home. The act of making a chair is also the act of choosing not to make a table, it is the decision to commit to one thing over all other possible outcomes. **Design is that decision in action and our approach to design can have significant consequences on the success of what we make.**

It would be strange to talk about design in the context of entrepreneurship and business without mentioning Steve Jobs and Apple. So much has been said about Apple founder Jobs and his commitment to design that repeating it here would be redundant. So, we'll skip all that and instead talk about mock turtlenecks.

If you've ever seen footage of one of Jobs' iconic product presentations during his heyday at Apple, you'll notice he's wearing jeans and a black mock turtleneck. Not just for that presentation, but for all of them. In fact, that ensemble became his only public attire. It became so consistent that if he wore anything else, it would have made headlines. You might assume that Jobs was simply defaulting to something in style at the time, that mock turtlenecks were a thing in the nineties, and he fitted in with mainstream culture. But there's more to it.

Mock turtlenecks—named because they are neither shirt not turtleneck—were not particularly popular at the time. It was not a great look. No professional stylist would have chosen this outfit, and it didn't particularly suit Jobs as an individual. Yet he wore it again and again, so much so that the idea of seeing him in a suit and tie or (heaven help us) shorts and a T-shirt was absolutely incomprehensible.

It is well documented that Jobs abhorred time-wasting inefficiencies and had little patience for the superficialities of personal appearance. It's true that there is something here about single-mindedness and operating at maximum speed and efficiency. But what is more useful to consider in this moment was his willingness to commit to a choice, to wearing the mock turtleneck and nothing else, and in doing so to optimize his opportunity to achieve whatever he set out to do. Whether he thought the mock was the best balance of comfort and coverage (why not go full turtleneck?) we'll never know, but the point is that he considered the possibilities and committed to a choice.

Contrast this with what you choose to wear, with what your colleagues wear, with what you see around you in your workplace. More often than not, you'll find that people mostly wear what aligns with mainstream culture. There is nothing wrong with this per se, but it can be constructive as we consider the value of design in what we do and how we organize ourselves as teams and companies. It's the difference between doing (or wearing) whatever seems normal versus committing to something different in the interest of a particular goal.

As noted previously, we think about design as an expression of commitment and a willingness to face the possibility of failure. In this context, design is distinct from art in that design is always purpose-driven and meant for use. Art stands on its own; it cannot fail for reasons outside itself, it exists to be apart from everything else and has no functional dependencies. Design, on the other hand, sits inside of human collaboration and action and can absolutely fail and fail spectacularly. This is the work of any product or platform and the difficult, painstaking work of making something perfect for someone else. It's hard!

Unfortunately, many of us only see or really consider design in the context of products or platforms. We marvel at the iPod and miss the lesson of the mock turtleneck. For Jobs, this commitment extended to every detail of his personal and professional life, and some might argue it reached the level of obsession. In Walter Isaacson's biography, he described how Jobs worried over every minor detail of his private plane, down to buttons on the passenger seats. Dissatisfied with polished steel buttons, he demanded brushed nickel—one of thousands of customizations that added enormous cost, delayed production, and no doubt enraged his manufacturer.

While Jobs may stand alone as a design zealot, far too many of us default to the other end of the spectrum. We wear whatever happens to be on the rack at the store; we work in bland, nondescript environments; we use cheap tools and make things that are safe and inoffensive. We avoid the conscious choice-making that produces design and differentiation and end up with unremarkable results. Design is the natural outcome of commitment, and if we seek transformational results, we must design who we are and what we do. Consider these principles as you reconsider design in your life and work:

1) Design yourself.

    No, this doesn't mean you should stock up on mock turtlenecks. Consider who you are and thoughtfully construct your personal appearance and actions to match. For entrepreneurs, this is especially important as having your team, your investors, your clients, and everyone in the sphere of your venture gain an understanding of the distinctive personality behind it is essential. It's extremely common to hear founders talk about all the ways they have to be and look and behave in order to meet the expectations of their audience. On the other hand, these same founders idolize, follow, and listen to every podcast from leaders who are truly and distinctively themselves. Consider anything you are wearing or using in your office and ask yourself: is this the way it is to optimize my personality and performance, or am I wearing it, keeping it, or doing it to convince other people of something that isn't true?

2) Design your team.

    Surround yourself with individuals who hold some sense of authentic personal taste and habit and actively work with them to cultivate it. Some of this is covered in the chapters on leadership and empowerment, but the point here is not to seek out people with flamboyant style or attention-seeking habits. Instead, look for those who have a vision for themselves and a sense of personal activation. From there, work with them to identify resources that would further optimize performance. If someone produces their very best work by coming in at 11 a.m., utilizing a standing desk, and staying until 9 p.m., get the standing desk and leave the lights on.

3) Design everything that represents your company to the world. The external materials and resources that represent you and your venture to the world require the same commitment and customization as you would want inside your office. After all, your audience only knows what you show them and this is the difference between communicating that you are perfect for something instead of available for anything. This is not about pretty and ugly, it's the difference between committing to choices vs. retreating to a place of vague, inoffensive blandness. Far too many ventures avoid bold choices and great design for fear of turning any potential customer or client off. In reality, they become everyone's third choice, the unremarkable option that seems to be available to anyone but urgent for no one. Invest in design, commit to bold language, and lean into what makes you distinctive.

The lesson of the mock turtleneck is not that you can save time by only wearing one thing, or that you can get away with wearing ugly clothes if you make great products. It's that you should commit to your choices and realize them through design and execution, even at the risk of putting someone else off. Jobs' attire didn't say much for his sense of fashion, but it said a lot about his approach to innovation and product design. We wouldn't wear a black mock turtleneck and jeans every day, but we were excited to have the guy who did design our phones and computers. His monomaniacal obsession to getting things right, as opposed to simply fitting in, was evident in his commitment to design.

How committed are you?

CHAPTER THIRTEEN

Accountability

In 2005, a trader at Mizuho Bank mistyped an order for shares and cost his company 27 billion yen ($247 million). He had intended to sell one share at 610,000 yen, but instead sold 610,000 shares at 1 yen each.

Whoops.

In 2016, Entertainment Cruises Spirit of Baltimore, with 400 passengers on board, crashed into a wharf during a midnight cruise in Baltimore's Inner Harbor. The captain had fallen asleep.

My bad.

We've all made mistakes, but few of us have made one quite so public or catastrophic as these two examples. Spoiler alert: both guys lost their jobs. But should they have been punished further? If so, what punishment would have been severe enough for these indefensible errors?

When we hear about mistakes, particularly ones that endangered or even cost lives, we start to think about accountability. In the common vernacular, accountability is usually intended to mean someone facing the punishment they deserve. It's a purely punitive concept and one that is primarily concerned with vengeance, retaliation, and just desserts. In the context of this conversation, we think about accountability a little differently. Holding yourself accountable and having those around you operate from a place of accountability can be a significant factor in overall success. And it absolutely does not work if your definition of accountability is swift and extreme justice.

The punitive model of accountability incentivizes individuals to hide mistakes or simply do nothing when the possibility of a mistake or wrong action arises. You know exactly what this looks like because everyone has worked (and many continue to work) in environments where this behavior is the norm. Personal accountability evaporates when being fallible means getting fired. Worse yet, this leads to a culture of scapegoating and blame shifting: it must be someone's fault, and it's not mine, so let's all join the hunt for the plausible perpetrator. This is where the real 3-D executive chess occurs—setting others up for future, as-yet-unmade mistakes, shifting potential blame, and positioning oneself to be left standing when the wreckage is cleared.

All very unhelpful stuff. On the flip side of all this, there is an equally unhelpful impulse in most of us to seek punishment ("being accountable") as a form of absolution. Wallowing in self-recrimination, these folks see punishment—suspension, fines, firing—as a way to reset the scales. Most of us can relate to this from times we've let a friend down and they were saddened or disappointed instead of being angry: we would rather be punched than pitied. Few reactions sting like a restrained, discouraged glance.

If we're going to understand accountability and use it effectively, we'll need to set aside these negative, unhelpful impulses. Avoiding blame or seeking punishment are two sides to the same coin, one that focuses on the mistake rather than what can be done about it. **Think instead of accountability as the means by which we restore what was lost to others while learning and growing in the process.** It's about standing behind what you've done and owning its consequences with the intention of using it to better yourself and those around you. It has three key characteristics:

1) Acknowledgment.

   Unlike the mistake-avoiding culture found in any blob-like bureaucracy, effective leaders and teams immediately communicate what they understand the problem to be and involve others in looking at it. This is different than confession for forgiveness. There is nothing wrong with that as a concept, but it has no use here. This is open acknowledgment of what occurred to any and everyone it affected, in an effort to truly understand what happened and what it will take to make it right. Effective acknowledgment is focused on the consequences for others, not the grand tragedy of what it feels like to screw up. Get over yourself and get to work in seeing how your mistake has impacted your cofounder, your team, your funders, your customers, and anyone else you put in harm's way. Doing this and having others see it in real time is the best possible means for teaching acknowledgment as a practice. Done sincerely, it will encourage others to do the same.

2) Restoration.

   Literally the opposite of punishment. Rather than concerning yourself and your organization with how the offending party will face the firing squad, you will see what it takes to repair and restore what was damaged for others. More often than not, reprimands and punishments simply create more chaos and bad feeling. Those hurt by the mistake are still hurt, the person who made the mistake is now hurt, and everyone who witnessed the whole charade has learned that they had better never make a mistake. Instead, seek out the means by which the stakeholders involved can hurt less or perhaps be made entirely whole over time. This could look like financial compensation, time off to accommodate the extra hours required to clean up the mess, an opportunity to restart a project that has been hopelessly derailed, so on and so forth. Show yourself and your team that your focus is on getting and being better, not channeling collective anger into "justice."

3) Reconciliation.

Having acknowledged what happened with a curious and open mind and having made every effort to address the impact of the mistake, you are ready to move forward in a way that assures everyone that the circumstances that produced that mistake won't occur again. It doesn't mean there won't be new mistakes—every dynamic leader and organization makes a lot of them—but it does mean that the people who depend on you won't fall into that particular hole a second time. They can proceed with the knowledge that you, like them, won't forget the mistake and have taken efforts to ensure it won't be repeated. From here, you can start over, not like it never happened but instead like it definitely happened, and everyone learned from it. This could look like a simple adjustment in process, or a significant reorganization in roles and responsibilities. Whatever it is, it should be a real and validated change that others experience instead of just hearing that "things will be different now."

Many high-performing leaders struggle to get past their own mistakes. They tend to be very forgiving of early collaborators and believers and in time, very hard on the later hires who weren't there in the beginning and "don't get it." This dynamic of being hard-on-myself, easy-on-my-cofounders, hard-on-the-new-hires is extremely common and indicative of a poorly considered comprehension of accountability. To others, it looks like favoritism or capriciousness, even outright insanity. Every leader and entrepreneur has to reconcile their relationship to mistakes within themselves and then to the people around them, irrespective of title or loyalty.

High-functioning teams do not have variable levels of accountability within them. Accountability is either embraced holistically or it isn't really there at all. Enabling someone who lacks accountability kills the concept for others and removes it from your culture. Restarting or resetting accountability as a team value is difficult—people may forgive, but they rarely forget. And their instinct will be to defend themselves from everything that comes with being culpable inside of an organization that lacks accountability as a core concept. On the bright side, a new relationship to accountability can begin any time, including right now. After all, it's not like you crashed a cruise ship or made a $247 million typo.

CHAPTER FOURTEEN

Empowerment

Can you remember the first time you rode a bicycle? No help, no parents, no training wheels, just out there riding all on your own. How about driving a car? Pulling out of the driveway and leaving your parents, your siblings, your very childhood behind you as you sped off to meet up with friends? Some of you have flown planes, sailed boats, raced motorcycles, and who knows what else. It was fun! It was intoxicating! That first feeling of freedom and power is unforgettable.

In each of these examples, you went through a process of discovery, proficiency, validation, and finally, freedom. We'll break these down in more detail later on but for now, consider the journey you took to finally get behind the handlebars or steering wheel. It's likely you experienced some fear along the way. You had someone helping you, someone who held power over the thing you were learning about, and would make some decision about granting that power to you. And finally, you experienced ownership of the power, the duality of freedom ("I'm outta here!"), and responsibility ("I'd better not see a scratch on that car!") that led you to independent action beyond anything you had experienced before.

Can you believe anyone ever let the teenage version of you drive off in their car? Imagine being your parent and watching your uncoordinated childhood self wobble out of sight on a bicycle.

Looking back and knowing how little you actually understood of the danger, isn't it incredible that it ever happened in the first place?

Imagining yourself in the shoes of the person who turned you loose on a bicycle or in a car is useful when we think about empowerment in the broader context of personal and professional relationships. This is not the empowerment you associate with having someone feel affirmed in their identity, which is fine but totally distinct from what we mean here. This is not the "participation trophy" of concepts we'll cover, some kind of soft validation that ensures everyone is comfortable with who and what they already are.

Empowerment is the force multiplier to any team or organization. To access it, you have to accept risk and truly trust the people around you. After all, you *really did* drive off in that car and anything could have happened, but in order to get what everyone wanted—freedom and independence for you, freedom *from* you for your parents—the team had to work together on elevating what was possible for you.

Let's break down the elements of empowerment to get a clearer picture of what it demands and what it can produce. This is the discovery/proficiency/validation/freedom cycle referenced earlier, a constant loop that should always be spinning with some varying level of pace between you and anyone you hope to empower.

1) Discovery.

    Believe it or not, there was a time when you knew nothing about that thing you eventually wanted so badly. Bicycle, car, sole budgetary discretion over a big initiative for a multinational corporation, it's all the same. These are things that you were eventually exposed to and over time saw as possibilities for yourself. And with many of those things, especially the ones that really mattered, it is likely that you didn't recognize them as possibilities for you the very first time you were exposed to them.

Anything that brings the real reward of empowerment with it—freedom—is by definition risky. You might succeed, and you might fail, but whatever the outcome, it was yours and yours alone to determine. Taken to a grownup, high-stakes, professional context, that's an intimidating prospect for many of us. And this brings us to a big misconception about empowerment. Some people see empowerment as "letting people have the power and authority they want." In reality, empowerment usually begins with *having people see they are ready for the power and authority that is available to them.*

That's discovery! From the leadership side, it means delivering enough transparency and organizational exposure so team members can see bigger challenges and explore the possibility of tackling them. Doing this in a way that is safe and thoughtful will aid in the demystification of these challenges and prepare individuals to take on the risk of accepting them. If your parents tossed you the keys to their car when you were nine years old, you likely would have tossed them right back. Forcing you to learn to drive before you were interested or ready not only would not have produced a good driver, but likely would have manifested a driving phobia that delayed or prevented driving altogether. Letting you ride around with them in the car, answering your questions about driving, and eventually letting you apply for a learner's permit made you into the enthusiastic driver you are today.

[BIG PARENTHETICAL BREAK: Some of you absolutely would have tried to drive at nine years old and are struggling to relate to this. Be patient. Your relationship to risk is unusual and all the more reason to consider how others experience it. Many managers and leaders have high thresholds for risk tolerance and struggle with empowerment *for this exact reason*. They keep throwing the keys at every nine-year-old in the building and get angry when all the keys come flying back at them. This is because their people aren't wired like them.]

2) Proficiency.

This is the part where an individual actually learns, in a safe and trusting environment, how to do the thing they will eventually be empowered to do on their own. In some cases, a person is just ready to take over the leadership of their team and it's best to simply step back and let them have it. More often, that person needs a transitional phase of guidance before experiencing the true freedom of empowerment.

Unfortunately, this proficiency training phase breaks down or is skipped altogether, not because it was impossible to learn but rather because the individual or organization in power never really intended to empower them in the first place. When faced with an opportunity for growth in leadership, power or influence, look closely at the preparations of those granting it to you. Are they really preparing you as though you were about to drive off in their car, or do you get the sense they plan to be in the passenger seat at all times to keep an eye on you?

The empowerment we're talking about, the kind that really makes a difference and moves organizations forward, recognizes the real freedom of the empowered and takes every effort to make sure they don't crash the car. Taking the time and effort to show your team member or directly report how to do something—and confirming they understand it—demonstrates the seriousness of your commitment to them in a way that your words alone never will. So teach them how to drive like you and expect them to drive off on their own (in your car) someday.

3) Validation.

As we've seen in the chapters on power, accountability, and other parts of this conversation, publicly declaring and affirming something creates a significant impact. In this case, it signals the freedom you intend to the empowered individual to everyone who will encounter that freedom. This is where the process moves into a recognition of the positives and negatives others might experience as a consequence of your actions.

In our driving analogy, this is the license that affirms you have passed a driving test administered by an unbiased (not your parents) third party. This process proves to the rest of us that it is reasonably safe to take to the roads with you and this is the thing that would be taken away if you proved yourself incompetent.

In a business context, we don't have the same cut-and-dried affirmation for promotions and changes of authority. There are no shortage of degrees and accreditations (no harm in them, but not much good either as it relates to this topic) but little in the way of objective, verifiable qualifications testing. What we do have is your presence and word as a leader that an individual is ready to take on a challenge and you trust them to succeed. Let the team see you hand over the keys and walk away from the car.

4) Freedom.

Finally, we get to the point of the whole concept. Empowerment is a path and process to freedom and without freedom, it is utterly meaningless. Empowerment is all about granting (or creating access to) power to someone else.

For leaders committed to empowering others, this final stage is a constant test of your commitment to outcomes instead of perceptions. Empowering people will teach you over and over, in myriad ways, that people can do things very differently than you would have and produce outstanding results. If your goal was to grow revenue by 50 percent and Kevin hits that target without using your advice, can you live with that? If not, review the chapter on leadership and think about what's happening for you. If it's all about being in control or looking like you have control, there is something else to confront that precedes your ability to empower others.

In a healthy environment, the journey of empowerment continues all the time. It varies by person, it varies by pace, but it is never neglected and in fact defines your interactions with team members. In time, it becomes foundational culture and (in part) sustains itself, but it begins with you and requires the courage and commitment to really let go.

CHAPTER FIFTEEN

Strategy

"What were you thinking?". This isn't really a question, it's an indictment. Something has failed spectacularly. The questioner is pointing out that you didn't actually have a strategy and you didn't think through the complexities of the situation or follow the possibilities of your actions to their logical ends.

Simply put, a strategy is a method of doing something, conceived prior to action taking place, to achieve an overall aim. That "prior to" part is critical. Wandering into the wrong lane of traffic and then veering out of the way of an oncoming vehicle is not a strategy, it's a reaction. Sticking to the right side of the road as part of a strategy to drive from Charleston to San Francisco is the prior thinking that would have prevented anything bad from happening in the first place. The overall aim— drive to San Francisco—is the other critical piece. Let's break this down along with a couple of other key terms:

Strategy: a method of action designed to achieve a major or overall aim.

Example: Jon and Chris will drive to San Francisco.

Plan: a detailed proposal for doing or achieving something.

Example: Jon and Chris will drive to San Francisco from Charleston in a rental car. Jon will drive the car while Chris gives directions. We plan to reach San Francisco in five days.

Tactics: a series of actions or steps taken in order to achieve a particular end.

Example: Jon will pick Chris up at his office in Charleston. Jon will drive safely and in recognition of all applicable laws and regulations. Jon and Chris will periodically stop for food, fuel or immediate personal needs. Jon and Chris will set the air conditioning according to a compromise between the two on reasonable levels of comfort. They will listen to music on occasion, converse on occasion, and sometimes drive in silence.

Our focus for the moment is on strategy, an intellectual exercise designed to create a desired outcome and the series of actions or steps to be taken in order to achieve it. We are not talking about planning or tactics, or the granular activities that fall within professional expertise, personal discretion or related to unknown factors that cannot possibly be predicted in advance.

The vast majority of strategies, both for individuals and companies, are fundamentally flawed. Most often this is because strategy is misperceived as a linear exercise. The San Francisco example works well because Jon and Chris originate from a fixed position in an effort to reach a fixed location. In real life, human psychology and circumstantial factors usually defeat this type of planning.

For most companies, and in all likelihood the individual reading this right now, the metaphorical car is already in motion. Whatever you have set out to do is in some stage of happening and you must reconcile this with your thinking. It has, in effect, been on the road for some time. Moreover, most individuals and organizations struggle to determine the exact location, direction, and speed of the car. This is a common challenge in strategy development.

The challenge is compounded by the natural incentive in those around you to perpetually represent the car as headed in the right direction in an effort to protect jobs and reputations and to avoid conflict. And that is why we see strategic plans to go to San Francisco (says so right on the title slide!) while in reality the car is driving toward Los Angeles. Both are West, both are in California, but they represent very different outcomes. Most strategies fall victim to one or more of the challenges below:

1) Confusion or disagreement over the destination.

    Are we building the company to sell it in five years? Are we a product company that sells a few services or a professional services company with a product or two? Are we aiming to be the best at innovation or quality execution? In any of these scenarios, the team has (in effect) been encouraged to just keep driving and we'll figure it out on the road.

2) Confusion over who (or what) is navigating.

    Do we drive by the map the founders presented during our capital raise? Are we steering based on our funder's gut? Are we simply chasing revenue wherever we can find it, careening from spot to spot? This leads to conflicting justifications for behavior, frustration over lost time and effort, and day-to-day arguments over which way to go.

3) Not enough fuel in the tank.

    This is where planning is out of touch with resources and has charted a course the team cannot possibly reach, given what they have at their disposal. When this is in play, staff are incentivized toward short-term planning ("Let's stop for gas right now!") instead of long-term outcomes.

Enough with the car analogy. It's out of gas. As we've already seen, planning is not a linear process, nor does it neatly follow the rules of the road. A better example might be a sailing ship at sea powered by wind instead of a motor. With this picture in mind, we can now benefit from a better model for planning in the real world—an asymmetric (or nonlinear) environment. The steps for such planning are as follows:

Step 1: Find your position.

Any individual or company must identify the important Key Performance Indicators (KPIs) and the right ratios or relationships between them. The obvious analogy here is celestial navigation. When in motion, an object must find a series or combination of fixed positions from which to determine its own location. If you are shipping software products, what is the relationship between speed of development and cleanliness of code? How much do you value innovation at the expense of near-term customer satisfaction? Consider your own priorities and listen to your team to understand the prioritization that guides their behavior. This will reveal where you are and enable you to identify a goal.

Step 2: Set a destination.

It must be more specific than "west" or "California." Find the latitude and longitude of where you and/or your company should go within a given period of time and commit to it. One of the most significant factors in organizational commitment to a goal is clearly defining what you are willing to sacrifice to get there. This creates authentic engagement from the people you'll rely on to get there. If they experience your destination as a requirement to be in two places at once, or that they will be punished for pausing anything else in order to get to where you want to go, you won't have complete buy-in.

Step 3: Assess the crew.

Do we have too few competent sailors? Too many devoted to redundant activities? Is anyone missing entirely? This step is virtually impossible without the steps that precede it. Having clarified what you are doing today and where you want to be in a year, a model emerges that can clearly identify needs and vulnerabilities.

Step 4: Respect the sea.

Storms happen. The wind can die away. The crew can fall ill. Consider the factors beyond our control that can influence the plan.

Step 5: Sail away!

Take your position at regular intervals and course-correct as needed.

Finally, a strategy must be simple and straightforward if it is to have any hope of success. If anyone has difficulty remembering the strategy, or explaining it, or needs to refer to the strategy deck in order to discuss it coherently, you don't have a strategy. You have word salad masquerading as strategy in order to check a box. It's the difference between "leveraging best-in-class technology and regional client services to become a leading SaaS solution for SMBs in the Southwest" and "doubling our revenue in Arizona by opening an office in Scottsdale." We're not saying the office in Scottsdale will necessarily lead to your revenue goal, but it is at least a comprehensible way of doing something that can be proven or disproven over time. And that, as much as anything else, is what strategy is all about.

Right or wrong, you'll at least be able to tell people what you were thinking.

CHAPTER SIXTEEN

Urgency

If you've ever been to a Department of Motor Vehicles (DMV) office, odds are you experienced something that you would not describe as "fast." No disrespect to the fine men and women who work there, but DMVs are famously slow. Throughout this book we've discussed any number of concepts that get things done but we haven't talked about getting things done quickly. Not in a hurried, anxious or sloppy way, but from a place that is committed, motivated, and enthusiastic.

You don't have to spend a great deal of time inside a DMV office to notice the absence of almost everything discussed in this book. But if you happen to be there near closing time, something magical happens (this magic act varies by state and location, so it may not occur near you but rest assured, it happens at most of these offices). Bound by policy process and by every customer who took a number before the office closes, the staff move into high gear. And we mean extremely high gear. Previously unseen employees pour out of the back rooms, every single customer service station opens up, instructions are shouted across the room, and people get moving. Some of you are nodding along because you knew this trick and only go late in the day. Others are upset because you thought getting in line early was smart (it's not). Regardless, closing time at most DMVs produces something worth exploring in the rest of this chapter: urgency.

Urgency is moving forward at the maximum pace of progress, a state of being that naturally occurs when other important factors are already in place. It is focused on the next outcome, not 5 p.m. or Friday or December 31st or whenever complacent people stop pretending to care.

In the context of getting important things done, urgency is distinct from a few other closely related ideas, such as excitement or fear. The fine folks of the DMV get in gear because they want to get out of there. This is excitement out of anticipation for a reward and it has severe limitations. This state of being does not contribute to overall elevation of the performance of the DMV, nor does it lead to innovation in service methodology or process. It is extremely self-interested and simply produces a burst of frantic activity that gets a lot of folks out the door at the end of each day. In like manner, fear of imminent punishment can get people moving quickly. Having a sales staff know that the rep with the fewest completed calls at the end of the day will get fired usually has folks dialing like crazy. It will not, however, create quality interactions that serve the long-term interests of the company or the customer.

Unfortunately, most workplaces operate somewhere between complacent, excited, and afraid. Or a regular rotation between those three states of being. It becomes obvious when you notice the attention given to arrival and departure times, deadlines, progress reporting, incentives, and punishments. All of these tools are intended to move people to action because it is assumed that stasis (inaction) is the natural state of being. Most leaders and managers believe that people must be prodded, bribed, and monitored closely in order to produce results.

Urgency is a condition to look for that affirms the presence of other important concepts. You don't teach urgency. It's not something to encourage or applaud, yet it's a critical factor to consider in what it can reveal by its presence or absence. Looking for it in your own life and career as well as the performance of anyone you manage is extremely useful.

The first characteristic confirmed by a sense of urgency is commitment. It is worth emphasizing how much a lack of commitment can slow someone down. Uncommitted individuals spend a lot of time observing others to compare and weigh their options, mimic productive behavior, and wallow in internal anxiety and self-doubt. Rather than shutting off distractions to reach maximum productivity, individuals lacking commitment to their role or their organizations seek out distraction and busyness at the expense of productivity.

Consider the possibility of working remotely for a week, away from Slack and email, to complete a business plan or code a website. This involves declaring to others what you will focus on, that you will do it to the exclusion of all else, and that you have committed yourself to completing it in a defined time frame. The vast majority of managers and leaders would enthusiastically support this (imagine knowing you would get a huge deliverable completed on time?) yet many professionals avoid this exact scenario. Why? Because they rely on the distractions and excuses to cover their lack of commitment. This could be due to a perceived lack of training or readiness for the task at hand, fear of failure in the outcome, or a lack of self-discipline that has them questioning whether or not they would use the week productively. Regardless, true commitment has people attacking their next goal, not avoiding it with disclaimers and excuses.

The second characteristic revealed through urgency is motivation. As noted elsewhere, motivation as we see it is not the same as bribery or coercion. It lives in co-creation, empowerment, and holding a sense of possibility for yourself and your team. Many, many professionals see a decline in urgency as they become uncertain in their relationship to their leaders, business partners, colleagues, investors, etc. Operating without a sense of clarity on those relationships and how they serve all parties leads to a lot of time and effort spent on negotiating (and sometimes litigating) the terms of success. It's entirely possible to be committed to a role or outcome and yet lack the motivation to attack it because you are out of alignment with others involved in that success.

Finally, urgency is an accurate measurement of enthusiasm. This is a sense of joy in the thing itself, fun and fulfillment in what you are doing as you are doing it, and not merely for the prize at the end. This appears to be in very short supply at the DMV, where the period of greatest activity is sparked by the prospect of getting out of there. In contrast, most Chick-fil-A locations appear to run on pure enthusiasm. With an extremely picky franchisee selection process, thorough training, and excellent compensation, Chick-fil-A populates its fast-food stores with leaders who actually appear to enjoy being there. In turn, they hire and train from the same mindset and create environments of infectious enthusiasm. Now tell me which job is more glamorous—taking a driver's license headshot or mopping up fried chicken grease? You wouldn't know it from the enthusiasm of the individuals involved.

If you've spent time with other chapters of this book, you've probably noticed that this one is a little bit different. For starters, we've indicated that urgency is not something you can learn or practice, but something that naturally occurs. It is or it isn't.

Moreover, the characteristics revealed by urgency are obtainable by anyone, even if they lack a sophisticated grasp of leadership, power or collaboration. Any individual or group can operate with urgency and no one can claim that a sense of urgency is beyond their reach.

The simplicity of urgency is what makes it such a damning lesson for individuals and organizations. We all know it when we see it and it is impossible to claim urgency when it isn't really there. You can recall a sense of urgency when you and your friends planned that golf trip; it was clearly there in the early days of your startup, you felt it when you were preparing your house for the arrival of your first child. But now you don't. It's gone, and you know it, and it can be hard to admit.

Rather than dwell on the negativity that flourishes in complacency, consider the components of urgency and build (or rebuild) the pieces that produce it. Fight the urge to tell others to hurry up, or bribe them into activity, and consider why they aren't attacking their goals. The answer will unlock an organization that no longer cares about working hours, progress reports, and arbitrary deadlines. It will move with urgency, speeding along at the maximum pace of progress, free from the games and delaying tactics of the complacent.

The end of day activity at the DMV is proof of what was possible from the moment they opened. Manage yourself and your team accordingly.

Concepts you work on within groups

As a society, we rely on osmosis more than we think. Ideas are disseminated through a careless process of proximity, where new people in an organization learn by literally being near enough to the veterans to mimic their behavior. We've been forced to learn on the fly; we've all noticed younger colleagues staring at us, trying to figure out what to do. It doesn't have to be this way.

This section shares concepts that can be communicated and implemented at scale. They can be disseminated a little differently than some of the previous concepts and offer the flexibility for groups to find their own relationships to them. This stage—the scaled and growing stage—can be daunting for any leader committed to maintaining the principles discussed in this book. After all, they can't personally explain everything anymore, they can't model all the behavior, and they have to trust others more than ever. It's tough. At the same time, it can be immensely satisfying to see larger groups working in sync, defying the assumptions around group dynamics, and performing at a high level.

So, grab a microphone and make sure everyone can hear you. These concepts are more important now than ever before and osmosis won't get it done. We believe in you.

CHAPTER SEVENTEEN

Competition

Is it possible to "win" at business? It certainly seems possible to lose. Ventures fail, investment dollars are never repaid, people get fired, etc. Almost all of us have had the experience of driving home from the office with a feeling that was very far from winning. And if we're honest, most of us felt like we, as individuals, had lost. We had come in second, or seventh, or worse and simply couldn't keep up with our competitors.

A quick glance at the business magazines and books in any airport bookstore seems to confirm this dynamic. Winners, often literally described as such, adorn the covers of magazines and sit atop rankings of the best at this or that. They won the year, the category, the job, the raise, the whatever. Hyper-competitive language defines and explains what happens in business and every analogy seems to involve sports or war. Western societies have framed business as a zero-sum game between individuals, where winners earn fame and fortune, and losers are condemned to shame and eventual anonymity.

This way of seeing and interpreting business is so commonplace and entrenched that often we don't even notice it. Moreover, the psychology of interpersonal competition seems to produce results. We all want to win, and we all fear the agony of defeat, so we're all motivated to do our best and produce results. Right?

Wrong. Completely wrong. The narrative of individual winners and losers is a lazy way to consider the contributions of complex networks of hardworking individuals. It's useful as a tool to sell magazines and books but a terrible way to frame your impact on the world around you. It fosters toxic relationships inside your team, shifts the focus away from the things that really matter, and sets you toward a goal you can never achieve. After all, someone else will always eventually win. The game never ends. Seeing business as interpersonal competition guarantees you will eventually experience defeat.

We see competition as the comparison of success for concepts that closely resemble each other in their intention, background, and surrounding circumstances. Note that we see it as competition between concepts, not people. While most professionals will politely nod and play along with this description, internally they hold competition as existing between individuals, ways of measuring who is smarter, faster, more innovative, and so on. While this is natural and will come up for just about anyone, the key is to recognize it for what it is and set it aside as unhelpful to whatever you are trying to get done.

Our experience in starting businesses and working with countless founders and funders has shown that commitment to concept—the thing that is bigger than you that can only be achieved with the help of others—is vastly more effective than anything designed to elevate the individual. And yet the temptation to see yourself (or your team) as winning or losing remains.

This is due in large part to the psychological consequences of risk. The risk any founder takes is much deeper than the superficial financial consequences of failure. Their venture is an extension of themselves, a public record of their capability to manifest what they envision. Starting something makes it a part of your story and identity, and how you perform in creating it will show everyone what you are made of. Or so it seems. It's easy for any of us to celebrate someone else's attempt to do something, to see their failure as creative and commendable, and to believe they will move on to bigger and better things. But when it comes to us, when we consider the consequences of our own failure, sphincters tighten and we quickly equate failure—loss in the competition—as a form of death.

Fear of failure in the interpersonal competition of business creates what we call the avoidance/obsession dichotomy. Some founders and leaders avoid the stress produced by the possibility of losing by operating in tunnel vision, refusing to examine the performance of their peers, and getting lost inside their won effort. The proverbial scoreboard puts them into a tailspin so they never look at it, preferring instead to play hard and hope they have more points when the final buzzer sounds.

Others take it in the opposite extreme. Under the guise of competitive research, they stalk their competition and consume every possible piece of information to learn more about them. Many, many of the founders we've worked with over the years have particular obsessions with rival founders—competitors in the interpersonal game—and hold unhealthy fascinations with what these other folks earn, where they live, what conferences invited them to speak, and so on. Many of you have encountered the founder or leader who suddenly suggests a product pivot, only for the team to discover that a rival founder mentioned something similar in a recent interview. Terrified of falling behind, the obsessive founder resorts to chasing their rivals. Both of these dynamics are bad! And extremely common. So, let's unpack some practical principles for productive competition:

1) Redefine success as conceptual, not personal.
    This means looking at what you have set out to do (launch an ecommerce sock brand, start your own law firm, whatever), and knowing that it (not you) is the subject of healthy competitive analysis. This one is easy to understand and agree with and can be exceedingly difficult to put into practice. For most of us, separating our own egos from the success of our ventures requires constant consideration and realignment. Your own personal success still matters. Be in conversation with your partners, funders, and team members about your own hopes and aspirations but separate them from the larger goal and understand that the two might not always be perfectly compatible. Your performance inside the concept still requires transparency and accountability. Finally, when you find success, know that others will still try to explain it in the conventional context of interpersonal competition. Just because someone called you a winner or you become the subject of obsessive comparison from another founder doesn't mean you need to fall right back into the trap.

2) Level the playing field.
    All too often, founders and leaders create comparative judgments from totally unrealistic competitions. They zero in on founders who look or sound like they do or identify rivals based solely on geography. Having a team member quit

to join another company can set off a burst of competitive fury despite the fact that their new employer does something completely different. Avoid these pitfalls by getting really clear on your concept—not your personal aspirations—and looking for anyone doing the same thing. From there, consider the circumstances around your competitor and look at factors like funding, patents, key partnerships, etc. Consider their methodology and leadership. In other words, go find an apple to compare to your apple.

3) Award points for the things that really matter.

These do not include snazzy new offices, what the founder drives, who was featured in a recent article, or what "lots of people are talking about." Use their product and thoroughly test it. Take a close look at who is funding it or trying to buy it. Interview their customers or clients to understand their experience. Read industry analysis and get a sense of what they are up to. Do they have an innovation advantage? Are they superior in customer support? Did their advertising blitz lead to a market share advantage or just paper over a bunch of churn? And remember, just because we've set your ego aside and clarified the nature of competition, it doesn't mean this won't hurt a little. Losing your fascination with a perceived rival may have you discover a scrappy startup that simply has a better product. That's healthy competition. Take it for what it is and get better.

One final point on competition: reframing it as a race between concepts can go a long way toward addressing unhealthy competition inside your team. The more you model an individualistic definition of competition, the more your colleagues will see the business as a game to be won or lost between themselves. It's a lousy way to encourage performance and leads to all sorts of issues discussed in other chapters of this book so let's set the sports and combat analogies aside and value what really matters—people working together in an environment of trust and mutual respect to make something happen.

CHAPTER EIGHTEEN

Agility

Every entrepreneur's job is to start a company that grows and then prevent the growth from killing the company they started, or so the saying goes. However you phrase it, bloat and bureaucracy are the obvious enemies of healthy operation, yet they appear again and again and again. Economist Ronald Coase's famous theory about management eventually becoming a drag on productivity was published in 1937, so it's not like this is a new phenomenon.[2] And yet it persists, even into sectors that at first glance appear immune by virtue of their design. Software development companies balloon just like consultancies, engineering firms, and retailers. Why can't these companies keep from getting so fat?

Between 1983 and 2018, the number of managers, supervisors, and administrators in the US workforce grew by more than 100 percent while the number of people in all other occupations had increased by just 44 percent.[3] Picture it: hordes of busybodies spreading like kudzu vine, swarming all over American companies to schedule meetings, swap memos, and borrow each other's copies of Dr. Spencer Johnson's *Who Moved My Cheese?*

It's a chilling thought.

---

[2] https://python-advanced.quantecon.org/coase.html

[3] https://hbr.org/2018/11/the-end-of-bureaucracy

We could go on and on about the evils of corporate bloat, but many others already have. Knowing that this book has caught your attention, it's unlikely you've set out to become an anonymous bureaucrat. Or perhaps you were dragged into that role and are ready to break out of it. Regardless, we'll skip past the obvious pitfalls of bureaucracy and focus instead on a concept we call agility. **Agile operation means every team member is directly connected to a terminal point of evaluation—customer, product or founder/leader.** Bureaucracy begins whenever an individual loses contact with what you sell, whom you sell it to, or the point of view that created it. That person is now feeding on the host itself, a parasitic organism that impedes fluid, flexible movement toward success. And we don't want that so let's break down the various means of maintaining agility in sequence:

Direct contact with the customer: Often limited to sales, support or other "front-of-house" disciplines, we encourage exposure to clientele for as many team members as possible. This can take the form of experience surveys, case study development, renewal/retention interviews, rotations through support teams, or drive-along opportunities with sales. However it gets accomplished, teams must have a present and personal sense of whom they serve and what it's like to purchase from them. Chick-fil-A, a runaway segment leader with revenue of $3.8 billion in 2019, is legendarily serious about exposing operators and managers to customers. You can own a McDonald's from anywhere, it's entirely possible to acquire one and never even see it in person. Chick-fil-A requires full-time commitment to one store and ensures you will have an up-close and personal relationship to frying chicken and taking out the trash.

Direct contact with the product: At Morning Star Company, the world's largest tomato processor, team members work with each other—without titles or hierarchy—and manage themselves. According to company policy, each colleague "will be self-managing professionals, initiating communications and the coordination of their activities with fellow colleagues, customers, suppliers, and fellow industry participants, absent directives from others." As a result, working at Morning Star is intensely focused on processing tomatoes instead of acting busy at Morning Star. Every employee is responsible for writing a personal mission statement that makes clear how they will contribute to the company's goals. They negotiate a letter of understanding with the individuals impacted by their work, everyone holds the power to purchase tools and equipment as needed, and compensation decisions are peer-based. And it works! Morning Star is an inspiring example of growth without bloat.

Direct contact with the founder/leader: This is more common in software development and consulting but attainable in any industry. It is decidedly not attainable at Walmart Inc., where more than two million employees work for CEO Doug McMillon. If he intended to spend just five minutes speaking with every Walmart employee, Doug would be talking continuously for almost 20 years. No disrespect to Walmart, but we doubt anyone would describe the retail behemoth as agile. We counsel startups and emerging leaders to grow headcount slowly and carefully, avoiding the crowding effect that takes team members away from their vision. Keeping your team closely connected to your leadership and point of view is a powerful antidote to bloat and probably the easiest of the three principles to maintain.

Put in engineering terms, agility is prioritization of function over form. Consider Tom Brady, the greatest NFL quarterback of all time, and the term he brought into the mainstream sport vernacular: pliability. Famously dedicated to preparing his body for the rigors of the pro football season, Brady and his training staff have developed a workout designed to maximize flexibility, functional strength, and resilience. He even uses it in high-tech sleepwear he co-designed with Under Armour called "bio-ceramic pajamas." It's an example of complete dedication to function over form. Imagine a Hollywood casting agent looking for actors to portray football players in a movie. They would be looking for large, muscular, imposing men who seem like they would play a violent contact sport. Form over function.

We're all susceptible to noticing what others have instead of simply assessing what we need. As we've stated over and over throughout this book, founders and leaders do what they do for a variety of reasons and compensation is relatively low on the list. For most, it's about proving someone wrong, propping up their ego, gaining control or accessing social status. All of these motivations hold serious risk for organizational bloat. They are all susceptible to hires that superficially aid in the work but in practice only add to the bureaucracy.

When we focus monomaniacally on the outcome we want to create instead of worrying about what it looks like, or what others are doing, or any other distraction, agility is much easier to maintain. In Brady's case, that agility helps him avoid 300-pound NFL linemen looking to take his head off. While the consequences of bloat might not be as immediate or personally painful to you, rest assured: parasitic bureaucracy will take all the energy out of whatever you set out to do. Stay lean and keep moving!

CHAPTER NINETEEN

Optimization

Peek inside any house or apartment in your neighborhood and you'll find an incredible innovation for ongoing improvement: a feedback loop. Close relationships in close proximity produce insights for, uh, improvement every day. If you happen to be married, this phenomenon will be even more pronounced. Governed by the assumption that you'll be together forever, anything and everything is under scrutiny for possible enhancement.

If you find this description a little humorous, odds are you are in a relationship that has achieved some level of health in its feedback. Others are groaning, feeling nitpicked, and examined to death. Either way, the key to the household feedback loop is its inescapable persistence. Simply claiming you'll empty the dishwasher won't get it done. Declaring that you will lose 10 pounds doesn't matter if those 10 pounds are still wrapped around your midsection in six months.

Marriage is in many ways a permanent focus group. It is the ultimate test of your usability as a human product. And it can be profoundly irritating. Anyone with kids, extended family, and other relationships in the mix might mention the pain of multi-demo feedback. Golf trips, spa retreats or any sort of break from each other produces a palpable form of feedback relief. Separated from the person seeking to perfect you, you are allowed to exist just as you are. Even if only for a brief period of time.

While there is certainly some humor in the domestic politics of day-to-day life, there are also a few interesting lessons we might apply to improving our performance and the performance of our products and services. First of all, many of us would concede (privately, if not publicly) that we are vastly better people due to the feedback we receive from the person stuck living with us. Left to our own devices, unexamined, our atrocious habits and shortcomings would run riot. Secondly, we would admit that the sheer persistence of the process produces accountability. It's not that I can't leave dirty dishes in the sink tonight; I can't leave them there *ever*. I have to become a person that puts dishes in the dishwasher immediately. Survival requires adaptation.

In a healthy and collaborative relationship, we might call this dynamic the process of optimization. The possibility for this optimization comes from a deeper commitment to getting something right rather than having it our own way. And while there will always be tension in that distinction, it's what makes our various relationships work. From this perspective, optimization of a product or an organization really isn't all that different.

Optimization is what occurs when a leader and/or an organization is willing not only to admit mistakes but seek them out. One that is willing to confront its own ignorance with a desire for healthy transformation. Finally, and most importantly, this search for improvement must occur all the time. If teams and leaders can operate from a place *trying to find out* instead of *already knowing and defending*, fast and effective iteration can take place at scale. So why do so many companies struggle with optimization? Shouldn't they all want to improve and succeed?

In the first place, most companies aren't very committed to their clients or customers. Whatever they may say, the truth is that they are actually just committed to *billing* their clients or customers. The internal psychology of companies that exist to invoice holds that the absence of complaints is success and further effort is summoned only when a client or customer threatens to leave (and becomes no longer billable). This is reactive transformation and it is the opposite of true optimization. This mindset produces incredible amounts of justification, rationalization, defensiveness, and inertia. Or, as we like to call them, the four horsemen of blob culture. This may sound severe, but consider the various places you've worked and the clients and partners you've interacted with. Odds are you've seen this firsthand and perhaps even fell into this kind of thinking while employed there.

The second reason is that they view optimization as a feature they can turn on and off. This looks like inconsistent QA before shipping product, occasional client surveys, a six-month "voice of the customer" initiative with findings that end up in a PowerPoint deck on a brand manager's laptop. While this is better than the pure reactive position described earlier, it still produces a lot of chaotic and unhelpful results. This is more common in organizations that still have some authentic commitment to the customer, possibly through a founder or dynamic leader, but haven't adopted optimization as a cultural mindset.

It's worth noting that optimization as we're about to explore it is impossible without a few other concepts discussed in this book. We won't repeat them here but suffice to say that any team that lacks leadership, fails to empower, and has no sense of destination will perform miserably at optimization. Seeking knowledge and exposing areas for improvement are deeply threatening to leaders and teams that struggle with the core foundational concepts of individual and organizational performance.

Back to optimization. By definition, this is a reference to improving something already invented or in progress and therefore distinct from innovation. It is the reexamination of something that you have already done in an effort to make it better and it is every bit as applicable to professional services as it is software development or mass manufacturing production. So, if you feel yourself drifting out of this chapter because you don't think it applies to you, know that it *extremely* applies to you and you might find more benefit from it than our engineering readers.

The keys to optimization are as follows:

1) Expand your data set.

   Most teams study a relatively narrow field of data related to true outcomes. These are great and will always be the bedrock of optimization research. But look backwards from the outcome to see what else could be timed or tested in the process that created it. In addition to conversion, or load time, or delivery speed consider tracking the pace of innovation, personnel combinations, and relationships between business activities and other factors such as workplace resources, compensation, cultural characteristics of regions where product is offered, etc. The first rule of optimization is to relentlessly search for more to optimize, never settling or feeling satisfied that you have asked every question.

2) Automate the analysis.

Artificial intelligence and machine learning have completely changed the pace and possibility of optimization and hold promise for almost any organization. If your company falls outside of a category with readily available tools to examine virtual relationships and transactions, consider software that can at least formalize and quantify on your behalf. Salesforce and other solutions can bring great clarity to so-called "soft" activities and interactions, leverage them, and make technology do some of the work for you.

3) Prioritize optimization so it doesn't compete with innovation or baseline execution.

Well-intentioned leaders can cramp optimization with unrealistic expectations for new products and features. Others simply place too many demands on operational staff to expect them to thoroughly review past performance and implement change. Unless optimization is held at the center of culture, it will be squeezed out by actions that (seem to) offer an easier path to recognition and reward.

Finally, let's not abandon internal and external anecdotal feedback. Simply asking your teammates and customers what could be better about a process or product can quickly produce some of your most valuable results. After all, in-person anecdotal feedback is what got you to stop leaving dishes in the sink. If you are truly committed to your team and your clients, their direct feedback will make a difference. Even if you don't always like to hear it.

CHAPTER TWENTY

Connection

By 1985, the executives at Coca-Cola were nervous. Pepsi, their rival for more than 75 years, was steadily chipping away at the soft drink behemoth's market share. Blind taste tests routinely favored Pepsi, even those conducted internally among Coca-Cola employees. Company chairman and CEO Roberto Goizueta chose to do the unthinkable—he would shelve the original secret recipe in favor of a sweeter version they would famously dub "New Coke."

Less than 100 days later, after fielding thousands of angry calls, plummeting stock value and watching Pepsi take the top spot in gross sales, Goizueta and his executive team admitted the obvious: they had made a mistake. Classic Coke returned and order was restored in the soft drink universe.

Remembered largely as a story of executive hubris, the New Coke debacle has another lesson to teach. Coca-Cola was clearly communicating with its customers. It had identified (what it thought was) the problem and was acting boldly to address it. Whatever you want to say about New Coke, you can't call it a cowardly move. Retiring the original recipe for perhaps the most recognized consumer brand in the world is, uh, bold in the extreme. What Goizueta and his team lacked is what we would call connection: a two-way communication model with customers that accurately identifies the real issues and the reasoning behind them.

From the flood of angry letters and calls they received once New Coke debuted, Coca-Cola leadership realized that their core audience had a far deeper relationship to their brand than they had ever imagined. Moreover, that audience was offended not so much by the new flavor as what they saw as cultural disloyalty. To them, Coca-Cola stood for something (originality? nostalgia? patriotism?) and to mess with it was messing with their values as individuals. After all, if you wanted a sweeter soft drink, that's what Pepsi was for.

Coca-Cola had framed the problem as a flavor issue. What they failed to realize is that it was a positioning issue. Pepsi had gained inroads among younger audiences by identifying itself as the beverage for them, not their parents. Coca-Cola had responded, essentially, by mimicking Pepsi's flavor. When the old recipe came back, now styled as Classic Coke, Coca-Cola drinkers came back in droves and eventually improved the brand's market share, all by virtue of its executives stepping on a metaphorical rake.

Coca-Cola had missed the point and misperceived its problem. It certainly had one, but because it lacked authentic connection to its audience, it thought it could taste test its way to a solution. And yes, this is a 35-year-old reference from the soft drink wars of a bygone era. But the lesson couldn't be timelier for founders and leaders today. Without connection, you are playing a guessing game, and you will very likely get it wrong—and you won't have an original recipe to bail you out.

Connection is an active and ongoing culture of open dialogue between company and customer that has leaders in touch—in real time—with the experience of their product or service. Early-stage founders tend to excel at this (or at least work very hard at it) by virtue of product or process development and the necessities of funding and audience validation. Having proven their concept and starting to scale, this commitment diminishes as individuals become more and more attached to their assumptions, salaries, positions, and habits.

Maintaining connection means holding the ever-present possibility of being wrong and needing to change. Most of us are inherently biased against this position, and it can take real effort to cultivate it in yourself, let alone across a growing team. Serious customer research has come on in leaps and bounds since the 1980s, but it is largely perceived as something for either the very well-funded startup or the very large corporation. For everyone in between, it is seen as an expensive luxury or something best handled anecdotally by founders and frontline customer service staff. Falling out of connection with your customers is prohibitively dangerous at any stage of the company lifecycle. Here are the key elements of connection:

1) Research context, not just pain.

It's relatively easy to ask a prospect or customer what hurts. Unfortunately, the answer will be very narrow and must necessarily be qualified by a great deal of assumption validation. Consider the Coca-Cola example—they ran more than 100,000 blind taste tests to confirm their theory that the recipe should change. By framing it as a flavor question and asking what hurt from that lens, they produced verified results that steered them in the wrong direction. Whatever your product or service is intended to solve, spend time with the target audience to understand the context of what they do and how they make decisions. Move upstream from the hurt to the fundamental premises of what they do and how they think about it. You'll likely discover that the hurt is different than originally assumed and will be positioned to address it.

2) Keep asking.

Great companies never stop researching their audience and build out smart technology to aid in the process. The more your customers understand that they didn't just buy a thing from you but rather are in active dialogue with you about the idea of the thing, the more information they will offer, and often voluntarily. In addition to the obvious surveys, focus groups, and direct outreach, smart companies build passive input systems where customers can offer thoughts without being prompted. More than anything else, this requires commitment from the top of the organization and real resources to make it happen. That means hiring a dedicated customer experience expert early on and arming them with the budget necessary to do great work and eventually build out a team.

3) Shoot the sacred cows.

We've talked at length in other chapters about the psychology behind the act of creating something and engaging others in it. Founding a company is no small feat, and frankly, there are easier ways to make money. Very, very few founders are truly and exclusively money-motivated and that same drive applies to the (hopefully) great people they surround themselves with to bring something to life. The pride and passion that goes into a company can unfortunately create commensurate attachment to original ideas and assumptions. We all want to see ourselves as being right. Some of us will go further, even in the face of obvious defeat, to prove themselves right as opposed to being willing to change. To many founders, changing means admitting you were wrong and it can feel extremely distressing. To avoid this, actively seek out products and processes and people you are invested in for reasons outside of the performance of the company. Let us assure you—you will find them! Don't literally shoot anything, but do the work to disentangle your own attachments with anything standing between your vision and the change necessary to achieve it.

To us, the New Coke story is anything but a hilarious failure. We would describe it as a glorious mistake, a bold action that took the company in the wrong direction. But by virtue of doing it, Goizueta and his team gained a better appreciation for what made Coca-Cola special and put the company on track for future decades of growth and profitability. They had the courage to act, albeit mistakenly, and the action produced the knowledge that did eventually get them out of the slump. Remember, Coca-Cola really did have a problem. It really did need to be fixed, and eventually they got it right. Far too many founders double-down on original assumptions and fight the wrong battles for years.

The Coca-Cola story is a failure of connection, not cowardice. We're urging you to adopt the mindset that would prevent such a costly mistake but rest assured, mistakes will be made. When they do occur, it's up to you to face your customers and clients and learn the truth. After all, no one is telling the Hansen Natural Sodas story (look it up) because it eventually just went away. Real leaders are committed to success through authentic connection to their customers, even if it means pivoting to New Coke and back again. And for the younger readers who are wondering: yes, it tasted terrible.

CHAPTER TWENTY ONE

Transparency

Southwest Airlines, one of the most successful domestic air carriers in American history, holds fewer than 20 patents. Several of them relate to onboard power stations for personal electronic devices; one is for route scheduling software and one is for the design of their provisioning carts for restocking aircraft between flights. None offer a clear advantage over any competitor; in fact, many are simply their version of what other carriers possess and have themselves protected.

Southwest almost exclusively buys their aircraft from Boeing. The U.S. Air Force trains many of Southwest's pilots. As it turns out, a multi-billion-dollar transportation leader and a company that operates some of the most complex machinery ever invented does not have all that much in the way of proprietary secrets. What they have, as first conceived by their legendary co-founder Herb Kelleher, is a clear and defined *way of doing things*. They found success with their Boeing airplanes and USAF pilots not through technical innovation but rather through process and execution.

This un-patentable position is true of the vast majority of companies not just in the United States but worldwide. Competitive advantage through protectable innovation— building a better mousetrap—is exceedingly rare. And in an information economy of open source, digitized, hackable intellectual property, even more so as time goes on. Yet, the secrecy myth persists.

The myth goes something like this: we will get ahead through invention and stay ahead by keeping others from doing what we do by force of law. It's a very attractive fantasy in that it frees the founders and funders from the burden of being better businesspeople. By creating a mechanical or technological advantage (and one that the public can't live without), the company can operate from a position of strength, fending off rivals without having to compete on a level playing field. Therefore, leaders and companies create things, keep their processes a secret, and hope to get so far ahead that no one else will ever catch up. And it almost never works.

We have signed more Non-Disclosure Agreements (NDAs) than either of us cares to remember. The secrecy myth is especially attractive to pre-revenue founders. Believing that a protectable innovation advantage will make them more attractive to investors and collaborators, founders hold their ideas very close. The truth behind the NDA is almost always underwhelming. Almost all of the pitch decks and business plans contain indefensible elements that others have already tried, rely on technology others have built or assume later innovations that are entirely unrealistic. We don't hold it against these founders. Some of their ideas were great and many of the entrepreneurs we've encountered are deeply committed to serving their target audiences. They have simply gotten caught up in the culture of secrecy that pervades so much of the discourse in business.

What matters most to us (and the savvy venture capitalists, who are way smarter than us) is what you see before the NDA hits your inbox. It's how the founder carries themselves and what they share about their approach to work: what they will do often matters less than how they will do it.

Which brings us to transparency, a word that most people associate with Saran Wrap or a public process designed to avoid the appearance of wrongdoing. For example, elected officials are supposed to be "transparent" about their work so we can make sure they aren't misusing taxpayer funds. And while operational transparency offers some useful trust-building benefits, we see it a little bit differently.

Transparency means operating in a way that maximizes opportunity for the customer or client by having them understand exactly what you do. Operating in this way also allows your competitors to see what you are doing and challenges them to beat you on the merits of your methodology.

Having your clients and customers truly understand what you do enables the possibility of partnership and co-creation of bigger and better ways of working together. Not every client or partner will be interested, some will simply accept what you have to offer and move on. But others will seek a deeper understanding of the forces guiding whatever you are doing and you should educate them! Better yet, let them watch you do the work. Show them the recycling facility where your product materials originate so they understand your supply chain. Let them observe your digital marketing results in real time through the client portal. Invite them to listen in on an advertising brainstorm session to hear all the ideas—good, bad, or ugly. You'll find them surprised and engaged by the offer and some will take you up on it. Those relationships will only improve as they see your commitment to a way of doing things.

Now about that competition part. Southwest Airlines has historically been known for superior customer service. Anyone and everyone can fly Southwest and write down everything they do. Anyone could, in theory, use their same gate announcements scripts, on-board greetings, in-flight updates, and deplane protocols. But if you did, would the customer still perceive it as outstanding service? The real trick to Southwest, if you could even call it that, is having (mostly) happy and enthusiastic team members: a happy team is a very, very difficult innovation to replicate.

Here's where transparency gets tricky. Committing yourself and your team to open and communicative relationships exposes unhappiness, careless processes, rushed production, and more. Poor leadership, stagnant wages, and low morale produces a bunch of stuff you would never, ever want your client to see. If anything, it only feeds the need for secret technological advantages (or claims of such things) to divert attention from other problems.

Herb Kelleher founded a customer service company that happens to fly airplanes. As a result, his company's success or failure never hinged on aviation technology. Consider what you are doing or intend to found or join. Now elevate the concept and ask yourself, what are we really doing? Consider the problem you are solving for your audience and commit yourself to that purpose irrespective of the technology you will use to achieve it. Molding your company's culture around that higher aim and not the widgets you produce will enable far higher levels of transparency for you and your team.

Finally, consider any and every aspect of your business that you regard as private and proprietary. Aside from compensation and personal information, is any of it actually protectable intellectual property? Could you pursue a patent on it? Or if you did, would anybody care? By and large, the parts of our businesses that we hide from our customers are the parts that don't fit, don't work well, or produce results that are unsatisfactory. Might it be better just to get rid of that stuff instead of hiding it.

Just because you can't patent something doesn't mean it isn't a significant advantage. Focus on real innovation—happy people creating great products and services—and you'll save yourself lots of time and legal fees.

CHAPTER TWENTY TWO

Mentorship

Some business psychology experts define a "senior leader" as someone in charge of people who in turn are in charge of other people. In other words, you would have to move down to a third level of the organization to find anyone who is primarily tasked with doing something that cannot be described as managing someone else. It's a useful distinction in professional assessments and human resource consulting, but you don't see it very often outside of that context.

For startups, this definition can also reveal the limitations of the founder. Unable or unwilling to delegate, they are trapped in roles as leaders (directly overseeing the doers) or somehow still doing some of the work themselves. As a result, the venture never scales and its full potential is never realized. For large corporations, it serves as a warning in the opposite direction. Too many senior leaders are an indication of bureaucratic bloat, the metastasizing effect of organizations that have lost focus and true purpose.

Regardless of size, most organizations struggle to define, improve or even hold an awareness of the human relationships within it. They are filled with people who self-identify as working in marketing, accounting, oil and gas exploration, chartered fishing tours, whatever. Their teams are trained to think of themselves as working on the thing (whatever it is) as opposed to working on each other. But wait—don't we all do annual reviews? Didn't we fill out some kind of work style survey at one time? We do March Madness bracket tournaments, host a holiday party every year, and remember most people's birthdays—so we're good, right?

Not quite. We've talked at length in other chapters about the characteristics of powerful relationships and the enormous potential in co-creating with others. We see it as a possibility even in larger organizations and would want everyone reading this book, regardless of whether or not you are a founder, senior leader, or a senior in high school, to know that *working on the people you work with* is every bit as important as *working on the work*.

We see this as mentorship, a conscious culture of working on (and listening to) the people in your businesses instead of simply working on the business itself. Mentorship is distinct from training as it is not primarily concerned with specific skills-building or the performance of a job-related task. **Rather, it is engagement with an individual to understand how they see themselves in their roles and within the organization, what they hope to achieve in their lives, and how you (the mentor) can help them become the best versions of themselves.**

Unfortunately, most leaders and companies only see mentorship as a possible side-benefit of training or organic internal relationships. Offering no formal guidance or space for mentorship to occur, a leader will occasionally take someone "under their wing" from natural affinity or political calculation. While it's always welcome wherever it appears, mentorship offers far greater impact when it is understood and implemented in ways where everyone can access and benefit from what it has to offer.

Our definition of mentorship hinges on the possibility that leaders can champion a future for their colleagues that goes beyond their roles at or within a given company. This is a willingness to be about something bigger than yourself and engage others who, through their ambitions for their own lives, can be a part of it as well.

As an example, a startup founder could connect with a colleague in a way that would enable that colleague to declare that they want to start their own company someday. This would be great to know! Operating from that ambition would unlock new levels of performance and deepen the relationship. The founder would know and operate from the expectation of eventual departure and the colleague would feel seen and appreciated for who they really are.

The other key point to consider is the power dynamics of the mentor/mentee relationship. Most formal mentorship programs operate almost like big brother/big sister initiatives, pairing individuals with widely disparate authority positions for something that looks extremely hierarchical and political. We reject this model but still see a necessary distinction between mentorship and professional peer support. As we understand it, mentorship necessarily exists between individuals with greater (mentor) and lesser (mentee) power within a given professional context. But as we've seen from the previous chapters on power and empowerment (*see also* pages 15–19 and 79–84), this would look nothing like a condescending coach relationship. Rather, this would operate in a place of enablement recognizing that both parties are, first and foremost, simply people and hold the exact same intrinsic value.

Keeping in mind the previous chapters on effective relationships within teams, here are three key considerations for mentorship as an organizational principle:

1) Unlock mass mentorship.

    It's time to discard the antiquated notion of mentor/mentee pairs. It limits the impact of your best mentors to just one lucky mentee and creates a host of unintended social and political consequences. A more recent approach, often referred to as "mentors-of-the-moment," involves everyone in a mentorship process that increases exposure, adds value through multiple viewpoints, and has been shown to produce better results for women and persons of color.[4]

    Leaders can start by creating mentorship moments with more colleagues across the organization and challenging their leadership team to do the same. They can fold mentorship into reporting, protect meaningful time for it, and conduct listening sessions to understand what would work best for the team. Unlocking mass mentorship as an aspect of culture begins with deep commitment from founders and leaders and will take hold when it is demonstrated—not announced—and individuals can clearly see its impact.

2) Leverage mentorship to accelerate internal innovation.

    Companies that commit to mentorship are well-positioned to create intrapreneurship programs, funded and guided tracks dedicated to the innovation of new products or services that otherwise would simply walk out the door. The justification

---

[4] https://hbr.org/2019/12/real-mentorship-starts-with-company-culture-not-formal-programs

for investment in intrapreneurship is obvious and well-documented: talent retention, organic R&D, team engagement, etc. For many companies the challenge lies in diagnosing and correcting the issues that make their existing innovation programs underperform.

Consider the previous example of the founder that discovers a colleague dreams of one day starting their own company. If that founder leads from a place that is selfless and creative and can connect with colleagues in a way that has them feeling supported as individuals, there is a chance for innovation and entrepreneurship within the company. When talented team members feel unheard, unsupported or unappreciated, it only accelerates their desire to leave and take the best ideas with them.

3) Learn to love your alumni.

Founders, senior leaders or anyone others look up to will experience some sensitivity around the departure of those they once led. It can feel like rejection, even betrayal. This dynamic has led many companies to operate from the mentality that *anyone who isn't for us is against us*. Former teammates are not welcome to visit or interact with the organization and their later success is seen with bitterness.

This mindset shuts down healthy communication about when and how to leave and contributes to abrupt and costly transitions. Great leaders offer space for colleagues to come and go, engaging them through the quality of their ideas rather than the fine print of a non-compete clause. We encourage leaders to hold healthy relationships—aided by proactive mentorship—that hold the possibility for change and can still celebrate success even after a transition has occurred. Warm relationships with "alumni" increase the likelihood that you will get great people to come back or, at minimum, benefit from their access and relationships as you continue to pursue your vision.

Imagine being a person who manages people, who in turn manage other people, and seeing yourself as anything other than a mentor. What a risk, what a mistake it would be to sit inside that interconnected web of human relationships and never devote time to the relationships themselves. We see mentorship as essential because someone else took the time with each of us to help us understand it. Who will you share it with?

CHAPTER TWENTY THREE

Curiosity

Curiosity is the necessary precondition for creativity. It's perfectly possible to produce action without curiosity, to give effort and march forward to a desired outcome. But it is impossible to be truly creative without the desire and anticipation for something truly new. This desire for the unknown is essential for anyone looking to make an impact and, in our view, can become part of the culture of a group or company.

To start, it would be useful to look at where curiosity comes from. **Curiosity is the natural state of anyone who understands the limitations of their knowledge and sees new information as worthwhile even when it contradicts their perspective or vested interest.**

The first part of the explanation may seem obvious, given that anything and everything can be sorted into what we know or don't know, but as we've pointed to in previous chapters, we all have a tendency to judge, assume, predict and otherwise act like we know things in an effort to appear successful or earn inclusion into a particular group or category. It takes a little courage and discipline to admit—even to yourself—everything you don't know. The more you can do this and engage others in active, out-loud not-knowing, the more you set the stage for curiosity and progress.

The second part of the explanation references intrinsic value, or the idea that knowledge is worth obtaining even when we don't quite know what we'll use it for. This varies by personality and background. We all know people prone to unplanned, hours-long internet research sessions and others who seem to take pride in the avoidance of new information. Most of us land somewhere in the middle, and that's fine—as we act toward our ambition, interest in random data will diminish and knowledge connected to our concept emerges more clearly.

In short: be honest about your ignorance and stop defining learning as a transactional process. Progress on this will unlock productive curiosity, a gift to anyone committed to making something happen in the world. In the context of this conversation, we see curiosity as the freedom to gather knowledge for its own sake in service of a goal larger than any individual associated with it. It is the abandonment of knowledge as leverage and the implementation of knowledge (and knowledge sharing) as empowerment and mutual advantage.

So now that we have curiosity, what do we do with it? How can we leverage it to our advantage? The first step is to trust your curiosity and actively work to maintain it as your life and career evolve over time.

Curiosity is easier for anyone starting out, anyone who hasn't been taught, doesn't have the experience, or can credibly claim they simply don't know yet. This gets a little trickier as we advance in our careers and start to have a vested interest in "already knowing." After all, that's what they hired us for—right? A college student with entrepreneurial hopes or even a pre-launch founder can admit to knowing nothing about sales, but what about the CEO of a four-year-old company that is struggling?

Admitting ignorance could be career suicide, clear evidence of unpreparedness, and a betrayal of trust to the funders and founding team.

Or so we think.

Abandoning curiosity in times of struggle and defaulting to "already knowing" as a position of defense against our fears is the death of creativity. In this example, if the CEO doubles down on the false assertion that he understands sales, it will only guarantee that the company continues to suck at sales. He'll create an alternate version of events where his sales genius was thwarted by meddling funders or market conditions or whatever and in the aftermath of failed venture, he'll be left clinging to one thing: that he never admitted to his ignorance of sales. It happens all the time.

Being comfortable in what he does and doesn't know opens up the possibility for curiosity, which in turn could lead him to finding a new hire that excels at sales. With the new business pipeline full and cashflow healthy, he can be Badass Startup CEO instead of Failed Startup CEO Who Definitely Understands Sales, two very different trajectories.

The other outcome of a continued commitment to curiosity is the possibility of embracing it as an organizational principle. When a founder or leader demonstrates a tireless interest in new information along with a ruthless willingness to admit what they don't know, it sets a template for others to follow. And it leads to simple, understandable explanations for why things work the way they do inside the company.

This brings us to the nemesis of curiosity, the timeless hallmark of its absence inside blob-like corporate structures: complexity. In most large organizations, complexity is where ignorance hides and thrives. It is the coded language of acronyms and jargon, the hierarchical game of keep-away, the exhausting barrier to entry for anyone who threatens those in power with their curiosity and ambition.

Founders, leaders, and companies should do things that work and should be able to demonstrate those results simply and clearly. Every organization will hold disciplines of great complexity within them, such as software development, supply chain management, etc. But the foundational reasoning behind those disciplines and the results that define their success or failure should be easy to understand.

Cultivating a culture of curiosity requires asking so-called dumb questions out loud to prove they are not dumb. It means challenging leaders to use simple explanations for activities and performance and holding them accountable anywhere complexity starts to creep in. And it means being prepared to answer questions from anyone and everyone in the company and if you don't know the answer, simply saying "I don't know." A leader's willingness to publicly not know something can activate curiosity across an organization and lead to solutions that never would have been possible without it.

What's over the horizon for you? What will happen if you really start creating something? What would the world look like if you moved past your fears and marched forward in joyful, curious ignorance?

You'll never know unless you try.

CHAPTER TWENTY FOUR

Scalability

By now, you've seen that we have a complicated relationship to business growth. We're obviously passionate about starting things, empowering people to connect with others, and making a difference in the world through collective action. At the same time, we're allergic to bloat, bureaucracy, and everything that seems to come with achieving a certain level of success. So how do we reconcile these two positions? How can we complain about companies getting too big while literally writing a book in an effort to help entrepreneurs and leaders think and act more effectively?

In a moment, we'll get to a specialized term definition but before we get there, it would be useful to remember how the dilemma got started in the first place. It begins with a person having a vision for themselves that calls them into action. They see a possibility for their lives and begin to act toward it, perhaps by reading this book. In its original state, this vision often looks like a desire to "own my own company," or "become wealthy," or "influence culture," or even some variation thereof. None of these ambitions are wrong or bad, in fact we see them as natural and extremely useful. And they all share one essential characteristic—a version of the individual that is greater (wealthier/more powerful/more famous) than the one that currently exists.

This is the fuel that makes everything happen. This fuel, when exposed to a spark of innovation, becomes the fire that drives everything to follow. Along the way, individual ambition takes the form of specific action or methodology. For example, the fundamental desire to be more could lead to enrollment in code camp, which leads to experimentation, which leads to application development, which leads to founding a company, raising money, and becoming a person that founded and owns an app studio. Success! Our example hero has enriched herself, accumulated some power, earned some notoriety, and become the bigger version of herself she dreamed of becoming. Or has she?

A funny thing happens along the way to fulfilling your ambition. The goalposts, once so clear on the horizon, tend to shift. What was once enough is now the norm (not enough) and we discover some of those same feelings from the beginning are still hanging around. This is the critical juncture for most entrepreneurs and leaders—the moment where they can either experience joy in ongoing creation or frustration in the endless search for enough. The tension between these two states of being is the choice between lean or bloat, dynamic and sluggish, powerful and merely performative. Some leaders scale their companies in service of the idea that is bigger than themselves (more on this in a moment). Others simply grow to grow, chasing the illusion that more people, more square footage, more customers, and more attention will eventually make them whole.

We should acknowledge that founding a company or immersing yourself in art or academics in an effort to outrun internal pain can be effective insofar as it can produce a big company, get you on a reality show, or earn a PhD. It can do stuff. It drives a lot of people, including more than a few of you reading this book. But in the context of founding something, it can make you particularly vulnerable to some situations that look like success but are in fact completely contrary to the concepts explained here.

The issue with entrepreneurship as a means of resolving internal issues is that it keeps the decision-making locus of the enterprise rooted in what works or feels good for the founder. Hidden under the veneer of competition or innovation is the desire to collect colleagues as a means of replacing family, to occupy larger, more visible spaces as a means of signaling success, to compete with others as a way of exacting vengeance for social disadvantage. And on and on it goes.

Founders and leaders that find peaceful, productive, sustainable success do so by giving themselves over to their ideas and their team, getting themselves out of the way and growing exactly and only as required in service of the thing itself. They seek the best possible version of the company, not as a proxy for their own psychology but as a separate organism with its own needs and wants and ambitions. From this position, they can judge decisions about growing headcount, real estate, investment in research, etc., and arrive at answers that are clear and defensible to others.

From here, we can see that scalability is the growth necessary to serve the idea and maximize its impact. The instant that growth overtakes impact, where something gets bigger than it actually needs to be to do its job, we consider that bloat and the beginning of the end of the original idea.

To anyone reading this book and considering the possibility of starting something, we ask you: is this about getting something for yourself, or giving what you have to offer? If you are setting out to get something, know that it is a severely self-limiting position and your venture is unlikely to produce enough of whatever you think you want to make it a joyful success. If, instead, you can see a possibility for yourself in giving something to your funders, your team, your customers, and the world at large, you stand a chance of getting more in return than you ever imagined.

This is why we wrote the book. This is why we are here. This is what we have to give to you. In all likelihood we will never meet, and whatever this book did for you will never make it back to us. But we don't care. We're passionate about activating and serving others from the knowledge that your success is more success, it does not diminish our success but leads to a world of more progress, production, and happiness.

Your gain is not our loss—quite the opposite. We see you as a powerful creator, a future founder or leader, a mid-level manager ready to break out, a college student with a bright future, a high schooler ready to change the world. And we invite you—we dare you—to go and do and be and disrupt and succeed and be everything you know you can be. We're here for it and excited to have played some small part in what is happening for you.

How the concepts go together

It's obvious that the concepts we've shared in this book relate to and depend on each other. No one concept is entirely distinct from all the others and each of them are aided (or impeded) by the presence or absence of other concepts at work. We could fill another book with all the ways we see these concepts overlapping and interacting but chose to break out a few combinations for closer examination.

Before you dive in, know that the water gets a little deeper in this section. It's the only part of the book that presupposes you have read the rest and in doing so, has us moving a little faster to deliver what we think each combination has to offer. It speaks more directly on outcomes and consequences and explores the possibilities that come from having applied the concepts discussed previously.

This section gets you a little closer to what it's like to be in conversation with us as we seek to hold each other accountable to a high level of performance. We hope it serves as a bridge to your own consideration and conversation, a place where *Spark* moves from teaching to something more like dialogue that you own with the people you count on. It concludes the book but for us, the work goes on and on. It's a pleasure to have you be a part of it.

CHAPTER TWENTY FIVE

Leadership/Strategy/Scalability

In recent years, the concept of "virality" has taken on a new and powerful meaning. Formerly it was limited to epidemiology and references to communicable disease, the term used to explain the nature and transmission of certain illnesses. Today, we associate it with a phenomenon like Wordle. The web-based word game created by software engineer Josh Wardle was launched in 2021 and within weeks had achieved immense popularity.

The short story is that Wardle created something intrinsically interesting and fun and through the power of the internet, tens of millions of people were able to find out about it and enjoy it almost overnight. It went, as they say, viral. The *New York Times* bought it in 2022 for an undisclosed price in the low seven figures.

Wordle is fun! Wardle made money. It appears the *Times* made a good investment. But a closer look reveals that Wardle never really set out to create a global phenomenon. He originally designed the game for his own amusement and that of his close friends. He was not prepared for its overnight success and countless copycat games. Wardle said that fending them off, "…felt really complicated to me, really unpleasant," and characterized the sale of Wordle to the *Times* as a relief.

It's entirely possible that you have never heard of Wordle, or that you are seething with indignation that the *Times* altered Wordle's algorithm to prevent the use of so-called controversial words such as "fetus" and "slave." Or that the game itself has taken on some entirely new dimension invented after the publication of this book. Whatever the case may be, one can see that Wordle's rise was largely unplanned, its success led to myriad unintended consequences, and its future is very hard to predict.

In contrast, **leadership** that commits to clear and specific **strategy** can access **scalability**, a concept we hold as distinct from the modern notion of virality. This is not a criticism of Josh Wardle or Wordle. Good for him and for the millions of users that enjoy the mindless fun of word puzzles. In fact, the example is especially useful given that you probably don't have strong feelings about it one way or the other so you can clearly see it for what it is.

The combination of concepts we want to examine here produce the opposite of the Wordle narrative. Leveraging leadership, strategy, and scalability as we've defined them here creates conscious, intentional, and lasting outcomes. Taken together, these ideas produce robust and resilient businesses, political movements, and even families. To understand how they go together, we'll examine them in sequence and see how they fit.

As always, the sequence begins with an individualized concept, something that happens inside of a single person. Leadership begins with the identification of something outside of or beyond oneself, a possibility that the leader can see and forms the basis of what others can organize themselves around. This is not a reference to clairvoyance; we are not asking leaders to see the future or predict every possibility. Nor is it a reference to manifestation, the idea that by simply believing in something it will bring itself to you. Our definition of leadership requires a destination, a future state that is real enough in the mind of the leader that it can be described and a strategy can be formed around it.

The first and fundamental principles of leadership confront us with a challenge. Those with a will to lead, who see a possibility outside themselves, who desire to influence and organize others, sooner or later discover the responsibility that comes with it. The story of Wordle, insofar as we really know it, is a sequence of events whereby that responsibility eventually became too great for its founder and led to its sale. Something that was never intended scale did so, and in doing so overcame the vision of its original leader. In the case of Wordle, this phenomenon is benign and even amusing, but a close examination of companies, communities, political movements, and even families that outrun their original visions reveals deeper and darker consequences.

Incomplete or ill-considered leadership can produce scalability, sometimes with startling speed, but without strategy, that scalability will inevitably devour the will of the leader or leadership team, leading to countless unintended outcomes. The first responsibility of a leader as we have defined it here is to lay out a strategy that guides outcomes and honors the responsibility of leadership. Truly effective leadership plans for scalability through strategy that ensures the continuation of the original vision and cares for the people whose lives will inevitably be impacted by the nature of the growth.

In his teaching on conscious leadership, speaker and author Jim Dethmer talks about taking "radical responsibility" for one's influence in the world. This is key in understanding the connection between leadership and strategy. A superficial appreciation of strategy would see it as an exercise in how I or we will get or do a given thing. A deeper interpretation includes consideration of what you will give (not get), what you will prevent (not accept), and how you will maintain a real and persistent recognition of what you are about while scaling.

Leaders accept responsibility and creating strategy is the first demonstration of that responsibility. When we strategize from a place of commitment and responsibility, the strategy takes on new and powerful dimensions. Effective strategy development almost immediately threatens the vision of the leaders because they force them to contend with the real-life consequences of what they envision. As noted in the chapters on power, empowerment, and co-creation (*see also* pages 15–19, 79–84, and 51–6), making things happen with others requires consideration of the rights, needs, and desires of others in order to maximize their performance. This must be woven into the strategy and in some cases, will act as proof that a leader ought not to move in the direction originally envisioned. In this manner, the strategy is the first safeguard against the leader, the self-imposed boundary that enables radicle responsibility.

The exact format or method of dissemination of the strategy can vary widely. Great strategies can live in notebooks, PowerPoint decks, planning software, or the back of a napkin. What matters is that they contain simple, memorable, and credible descriptions of how people will move together to get something done. We've all seen "strategies" that attempt to cover deep deficiencies with style or sheer size. If a layperson can't understand a strategy, it is flawed. If the strategy immediately begets questions around what happens next, the strategy is flawed. If the strategy focuses on avoiding failure but lacks specificity around how we would handle success, it is flawed. The good/bad news about strategy creation is that almost anyone can recognize a good one. Unfortunately, these are in short supply and most young professionals have never seen one. Rest assured, you'll know it when you see it.

Persistent frustration with strategies (or lack thereof) may be a sign that you yourself should create it. That brings us back to the responsibilities of leadership and the will and effort required to lead. Nevertheless, leadership *requires* strategy to produce meaningful, lasting scalability.

Powerful leaders that commit themselves to effective strategy development necessarily produce scalability. It is the result of the two concepts in action together. Scaling successfully requires the persistence of leadership over time through strategic action. Many organizations scale through two very different and very flawed models.

The first is something we call the Big Bang theory of growth. It valorizes a leader who "gets things started" but over time abdicates responsibility. These organizations are typified by frequent pivots, extreme sensitivity to competitors and fads, and a lack of thoughtful documentation that would enable others to truly understand or participate in the strategy.

The second is the Creator theory of growth. This positions the leader as God the father/mother, the all-knowing architect of everything that is obsessively involved with everything. These organizations are recognized by inflexibility, fear of disagreement with the creator, and voluminous documentation intended to deify and justify the founder's original assumptions and decisions.

Healthy scalability requires persistent leadership that adheres to the principles we've discussed previously, one that recognizes a leader's responsibilities while affording room for others to act and create. Note that we've used the term healthy, this is not synonymous with fast. While it is possible to grow quickly in this model, the speed of growth would live in the effectuation of the strategy and the necessary support and tools would be available to sustain it. Effective leadership requires strategy and this, in turn, leads to healthy scalability.

Wordle is fun and Josh Wardle deserves all the credit in the world for making something that millions of people enjoy. His story is also useful in having us consider whether we're being intentional about what we've set out to do. Playing Wordle is itself a guessing game, an endless iteration of not knowing what comes next. Your job as a leader is to see what comes next and prepare for it. The leadership/strategy/scalability dynamic is immensely powerful and taken together, it can accomplish anything.

How will you use it?

CHAPTER TWENTY SIX

Integrity/Co-creation/Agility

"Trust" is one of those interesting words that seem to require a lot of other words around it to explain what we actually mean. In many cases, it is a reference to one's level of competence to complete a task; no one should trust the authors of this book to help them fix their car because we aren't qualified to do it. With the best of intentions and every effort to help, we would fail. Therefore, in that context, we cannot be trusted.

I don't trust a hungry bear to leave me alone if we cross paths in a forest. The bear has no ill will for me, to them I am simply a meal. Perhaps the more accurate statement would be that I trust the bear to attack. That would be a fulfillment of its instinct and the most natural action it could take. I don't trust the law of gravity as that suggests gravity requires me to trust it in order to occur. Gravity, like all natural laws, occurs irrespective of my trust or lack thereof.

Do you trust your colleagues? When we move trust into an interpersonal context and attach it to collaboration and collective action, things get even more complicated. The answers are usually conditional and come with any number of caveats. Most of us talk about trust a lot and act as though we trust each other very little. We lock doors at night, sign contracts to enforce future behavior, withhold information, drive defensively, and stare at our home security camera feeds. Many people avoid certain places, have rules about candy or alcohol, and set alarms and reminders because they don't even trust themselves.

Taking the risk to start something big and build it with other people seems to require a lot of trust yet it is precisely because of this reliance on trust that so many ventures stall, go sideways, or fail entirely.

This brings us to **integrity**, a concept we previously defined as keeping one's word whole and complete—the idea that you always do what you say you will do and can be counted on to keep your word. This is a positive concept, not normative, like the law of gravity. You don't need to trust gravity because it simply is and even if we were to erase all record of its discovery, it would be rediscovered. It operates without anyone needing to agree on it. Normative concepts are impossible to prove scientifically and therefore require consensus.

Operating with integrity is a bedrock principle that makes most of the other ideas in this book possible. And it is absolutely required to achieve a high level of **co-creation**, the necessary mindset for two or more people to accomplish something together. Without integrity, there is no basis for co-creation as neither party would ever really know what they could count on from the other. If you've ever watched children arguing over who will do what in the monumental task of doing the dishes together and it occurred to you that it would be done by now if they had just gotten started right away, you have seen the perils of action without integrity. Each fearing the other will find some advantage, they argue endlessly about who will rinse, who will dry, etc.

If you find the idea of children arguing over dishes tiresome, I recommend against visiting most corporate boardrooms.

The dynamic is the same. Mistrusting each other's motives, the meeting participants maneuver for advantage, haggling over personal positioning while neglecting the issue at hand. This is mutually assured destruction, the opposite of co-creation, and this is where great ideas and products go to die.

Operating with integrity sets the table for co-creation and this, in turn, affords an amazing opportunity: **agility**. In our chapter on agility (*see also* pages 105–8), we offered the possibility of every team member having a direct connection to a terminal point of evaluation: customer, product, or leader. It's likely that our thoughts on agility sounded absolutely bizarre to some of you, particularly those with large team or corporate experience.

Teams and companies with low levels of integrity and co-creation cannot be agile. Our discussion on agility suggested a high level of independence for individuals involved in the venture. It maximizes the opportunity for asynchronous action by assuming all parties live in a context of integrity and co-creation. This is literally the opposite of most organizations where layers and layers of oversight are required to manage even straightforward initiatives.

So how does it get this way? Few would dispute the sluggish nature of most organizations, yet none would suggest that the various members of these corporate blobs *want* it to be this way or set out to create it as such. Is calcification the natural law of group dynamics? Does this just happen over time, like aging, and we cannot stop it? We see the erosion of trust and independent action as understandable and preventable. Not necessarily easy, but something we can prevent and combat.

It begins with a recognition of how most people were socialized and trained from early ages. Trapped in monolithic institutions (schools), young people are rewarded for adopting the language and behavior of responsibility while avoiding the reality of what it means to commit yourself to something. Consider the dynamics of a group project for biology class, a subject none of the participants are particularly passionate about. All of them are forced to take the class and must pass it in order to progress and eventually escape high school. This triggers a game to see who is the most afraid of getting a bad grade. That person will do most of the work in the group project.

Compare that to the very same kids gathered in a garage late at night for band practice. They play music for fun, chose each other as members of the band, and love the music. Everyone is committed and authentically seeking to contribute. There will be issues with selfishness and poor judgment, to be sure, but the real possibility exists for co-creation and agility. It is available because their efforts were not coerced into participating and they own the freedom to act and create. Same kids, very different dynamic at play.

This pattern persists into jobs and careers, mostly coercive environments where mistrust and responsibility avoidance can thrive. Most young professionals exit education to only enter a different kind of monolithic institution, a large corporation, where the same dynamics occur at a higher level of sophistication. Faced with an embedded culture and system far too large to influence or change, unproductive impulses become habits that over time, ingrain and define that person.

This is where some of them wash out of the mainstream employment machine to become entrepreneurs. By granting themselves the power to build their own institutions, these young professionals have the opportunity to design them with freedom and independence in mind. Except very, very few of them received training in concepts like integrity and co-creation—they were stuck doing group projects in biology. They know they want agility for themselves and their startups, but it is unclear how to create it so they begin with passion and energy (band practice!) but over time, fall into the same habits and patterns that formed their education. And another blob is born.

The missing piece here is radical acceptance and implantation of integral behavior. This demands emotional maturity and can be very challenging for some to attain, let alone maintain over time. The hardest work on the road to agility is being a demonstration of the integrity you need from your team in order to function at the highest level.

With integrity in place, (or at least at work), thoughtful language must be produced that brings clarity to the purpose and strategy of the venture. Co-creation comes from *alignment*, not *coercion*, and has to be grounded in more than enthusiasm. This means clear definitions of what we have set out to do and each person's role in creating it. From there, founders and leaders must be prepared to listen as the co-creation feedback loop begins to move, informing their own intentions and refining the collaborative dynamic.

Persistent, day-to-day focus on integrity and present participation in co-creation automatically produces agility. Observers will see that agility and assume, wrongly, that it occurs because you have a great deal of trust in your team. In reality, you have eliminated the need for trust by implementing a system of certain knowledge. Being with people in a way that has you know what you can count on, in a context where alignment produces independent action toward a shared goal, is the opposite of just trusting someone to figure it out. It removes that burden from them (and yourself) by installing the scaffolding that will actually hold the thing up.

Knowing something is very different than trusting it. And while we use the word "trust" to mean many things, focusing on integrity and co-creation will produce what we actually want from trust: agility. This allows for smaller teams that get more done and hold the flexibility to become whatever is necessary to achieve their goals.

It works. Trust us.

CHAPTER TWENTY SEVEN

Purpose/Accountability/Mentorship

In our previous chapter on purpose, it probably became clear that we were talking about change. After all, persistence of the status quo is not purpose, it is stasis, an entirely false notion but one that persists nonetheless. Individuals who choose to take charge of the inevitable change in their lives, who seek to act with intention to create the change, must move with purpose to generate results.

As a species, we're on the whole pretty uncomfortable with change. After all, our brains are predictive machines that have evolved to protect us. They do this by memorizing and avoiding threats, always governing our actions by calculating the perceived cost to our future selves. If we're safe at the moment, we have an impulse to keep things the way they are, given as we might not be safe if things were to change. This is the fundamental impulse that prevents people from changing jobs (what if it is worse?), asking for a raise (what if I get fired?), speaking up as a leader in a meeting (what if no one agrees?), and so on. We rationalize it to ourselves in a million little ways but ultimately, we are designed to avoid risk. And change always looks like risk at first.

Acting from **purpose** and accepting the responsibility of being a leader means you will create change in the lives of others. You won't coerce or force them to do anything, they will choose the change for themselves; it will come with all sorts of fantastic possibilities, but you as a leader will represent change in their lives and that will undoubtedly produce some discomfort. This is unavoidable if you are up to anything significant.

So, what do we do about that? How do we manage it and move forward with productive collaboration? The concept that most closely follows purpose is **accountability**, or radical responsibility for the change we produce in the world. If purpose represents change, then accountability represents the acknowledgment and acceptance of responsibility for the change.

Most leaders (and would-be leaders) would readily acknowledge the accountability they hold for their actions. What they miss is how the two concepts go together at the same time, in tandem, and must be seen in unison in order to produce the third concept in the sequence: **mentorship**. Purpose and accountability are inextricably linked and only when demonstrated together, over time, can a leader access the kind of powerful mentoring relationships you'll need with your team.

In practice, this looks like clear communication to others around purpose and accountability at the same time. Many leaders hold accountability as an unspoken possibility, the assumed virtue that will come into play if or when something bad happens. This view holds accountability in the context of judgment, that things will occur to team members as good or bad and that they need to step up and accept responsibility when a "bad" thing happens. In reality, your colleagues and co-creator's experiences are much more complicated.

We're reminded of the letters General Dwight D. Eisenhower prepared before allied troops landed in France on D-Day in World War II. He famously prepared two versions for submission to US command, one that attributed all credit to the troops for success and another that personally accepted all blame in the event of failure. The landing was a success, he credited the troops, and the rest is history.

As leaders, we yearn for this kind of clarity. Thankfully, we're not confronted with the kind of immediate and lethal outcome that Eisenhower faced when drafting his famous letters. Instead, our teams and followers experience change that often defies simple good/bad categorization. Moreover, as we saw in the chapter on objectivity (*see also* pages 31–5), that kind of categorization is limiting and unhelpful anyway.

In communicating our purpose and vision with those we hope to engage, it is important to acknowledge the areas where change is required and accept responsibility for the consequences of that change. If our purpose is to build something, and we can see a possibility of building it with you, we want to be sure that you can see the potential outcomes of what we'll undertake and experience full freedom in your own choice to participate. From there, we want to be with you in the experience of the changes in your life and acknowledge our role in how they came to be. Over time, as you move in alignment with us and shared purpose guides our actions, your own accountability will come into play and together we will share responsibility for what we have chosen of our own free will.

This is very distinct from a mindset that holds "if our startup fails, you can blame me." That takes the wrong lesson from Eisenhower, a hero/martyr view of leadership that skips over your day-to-day relational responsibility and only shows up when it's too late to make a difference.

Effective accountability would look like acknowledging that relocating to join a startup would require a team member's partner to quit a job and find another in a new city. There is no guarantee that they will find a job or that the one they find will be suitable. The startup is a risk not just for the team member but also the people they count on that that consequence must be considered before committing to the venture. This would produce a conversation about what would happen if the partner didn't find a job, the economic impact to the family, climate for employment in the new city, etc.

Can you see how that got a little bit granular and specific? Can you see the work? Internal or external proclamations about accepting blame for failure are often a means to avoid the real work of accountability in the act of creating something. Effective accountability is curious, committed, persistent and, at times, laborious and boring. Something else to notice from the example is that no one promised to find a job for the partner. No reassurances that it would "all work out." No offer of a bonus to cover expenses if the job search took longer than expected. These and other actions fall into the fairy godmother category of accountability, one that does not hold the team member to account but rather accepts all responsibility on the leader.

Being accountable with someone over time, and asking for their accountability in return, unlocks powerful mentorship that results in more than what was originally thought possible. We see mentorship as a relationship over time, a consistent presence is someone else's life that cultivates trust and elevated performance. To get there, we have to overcome the primary deterrent in the purpose/accountability/mentorship sequence: the avoidance of vulnerability.

A purpose big enough to require the help of others to achieve holds within it an admission: you can't do it on your own. This is the first level of vulnerability and one that many leaders avoid. They aim to attract talent and create teams while subtly expressing the notion that if you can't help, they will just find someone else who can. That the only irreplaceable member of the team is the founder and visionary. This compromises the purpose, prevents accountability, and entirely precludes the possibility of effective mentorship. Letting team members know you can't do it without them is a critical acknowledgment and the first important vulnerability hurdle.

The second hurdle comes with authentic, persistent accountability. Truly acknowledging the change occurring in the lives of others and the impact it creates has leaders showing up with empathy, being prepared to listen, and ready to own their mistakes. Admitting you are not perfect to someone you have already acknowledged as essential feels risky. However, the real risk lies in being an inauthentic version of yourself, unwilling to concede your flaws, and in doing so, creating distance between yourself and the team members you need to mentor.

Finally, successful mentorship requires vulnerability and emotional availability. Countless managers view mentorship as a hierarchical function, a transference of knowledge from the top down that occurs in scheduled, regulated instances. We see mentorship in the context of a relationship that would have a leader sharing unflattering experiences, learning from the mentee in areas where they need to grow, and occurring for the other person as someone who is truly investing in them outside of a transactional context. This work not only empowers the mentee, it demonstrates effective mentorship in a way that can be duplicated and become a part of culture across the organization.

Leaders with purpose create change and must be accountable for the consequences of that change. In doing so, they can become mentors and co-create their colleagues as better versions of themselves. But to do all this, they must confront their own relationship to vulnerability and be prepared to acknowledge that they need others, are not perfect, and can learn from anyone, especially their mentees.

CHAPTER TWENTY EIGHT

Destination/Design/Optimization

To the chagrin of our publishers, we have written a short book (you're welcome!). Our original commitment to each other was to create something without an ounce of fat on it, a book that only said what it needed to say, and acted as a demonstration of the concepts it contained. After all, a book about performance and accountability wouldn't land the same way if readers couldn't see commitment on every page. Whether or not we have succeeded is up to you, but the fact remains that we left a lot of stuff out. A lot. And that was painful.

Design, as we have discussed previously, is the final decision on what you *won't* do. There is a rambling, incoherent, 150,000-word version of this book somewhere that could have been produced if we weren't actually committed to the design of the book. It would be the version where we didn't leave anything out, where every idea was included, where all of our precious thoughts found life on the page. And it would have been terrible.

Accessing rigorous, successful design requires a clear **destination**. This is the defined, external outcome that guides your actions. It is the framework that determines everything for us. In our case, the destination is to spark action in the lives of our readers. This is distinct from seeing all our ideas on the page. If we're truly committed to a destination, that means we have to sacrifice some of what we wanted in order to design a book to fulfill on what we set out to do.

The connection between destination and **design** is fairly clear and if you re-read these chapters in sequence, the pairing will become even more obvious. Proceeding from destination to design opens up the possibility of **optimization**, and this is where it gets scary. Successful design means committing to something in a way that has it available for testing and refinement. It takes it to a place of rational consideration, where its success (or lack thereof) can be seen and proven. This is where many founders and leaders lose their nerve.

While the alternate, massive version of this book seems silly, we would have you consider the comforts it would bring to us. In its muddled mess it would likely offer something of value to many audiences. It would defy easy explanation and rest inside of an amorphous, hard-to-measure place of "good enough." If our destination was simply to see if we could get a book published, or to collect all of our random thoughts, or to simply say so much that anyone would agree with some part of it, we would have succeeded. Best of all, we would have avoided the possibility of someone clearly proving that we got it wrong. Its sheer size and shape would defy rational judgment and we would be safe from the criticism we naturally fear.

If the idea of a 600-page version of this book is amusing, consider some of the PowerPoints and planning documents we've all been subjected to. The meandering meaninglessness of strategic plans, fundraising decks, pitch presentations that cannot possibly fit inside of the 10-minute time limit for speakers. We're surrounded by would-be leaders whose destinations and designs are totally obscured by a lack of commitment. Fearing failure and rejection, these folks found safety inside a mass of words, charts, and graphs.

Our book is clear enough in its destination and design to be worthy of the possibility of disagreement. This is at the heart of optimization. Anything worth doing must be clear and committed enough to its purpose that someone else could see it for what it is and make some judgment around its success. Framing something as "worthy of disagreement" may sound odd at first, but for us, this is the first measure of success. After all, we have to know if it works in order to iterate and improve.

Setting the book aside, consider everything you are up to as you read these pages. Can you identify areas where you lack destination, and therefore have not designed, and as a consequence have no opportunity to optimize? This occurs all the time in personal efforts, relationships, and obviously in business.

If your destination is to get fit, you can design an exercise program and you can see if it results in something called "getting fit." This is where we can see a fear of failure *even within ourselves*, even if no one else knew what we were up to. Avoiding the possibility of failure is a deeply held instinct and can even prevent us from internal definitions and measurements.

If your destination is to enjoy a happy and healthy relationship with a partner, you could declare that intention and work with your partner to design the parameters of your relationship, enabling you to measure its success over time. Now we have introduced a second party to the equation and heightened the fear factor. What if they don't reciprocate? What if their definition of relationship differs from mine? And so we persist in undefined, un-designed connections with others, never achieving the happiness we hoped for out of a desire to avoid the disappointment of separation.

Finally, consider the big, meaningful thing you want to create. Maybe it's a startup. Now we have entered the arena of maximum, public possibility for rejection. Funders could turn you down, hoped-for colleagues refuse to join, the idea itself could be met with scorn. That would hurt! But you could learn from it and optimize your efforts in the future. It would provide a basis for improvement and enhance the possibility of future success.

We see the destination/design/optimization sequence as a loop, constantly testing and proving out whether or not all three concepts are at work. Undefined destination produces mediocre design. Going to the gym without a straightforward sense of what success looks like would lead to weird activities and results. Are we there to lose weight? Build muscle? The workouts would be incoherent and therefore impossible to judge. Poor design defeats optimization—it is impossible to improve on something if it cannot be measured—and that should have us circling back to reconsider the purpose.

The last piece of the optimization challenge is to push through to a state of permanent iteration. Having overcome the fear of rejection and designed with commitment, it's possible you could enjoy a measure of success with your workouts, your relationship, or your startup. The temptation to rest on that success is immense. After all, isn't that the reward for what you've just been through?

The highest level of optimization is a full and radicle embrace of permanent iteration. It is a rejection of the mountaintop theory of progress, one that holds the idea of arrival at a peak that affords a resting place from the discomfort we seek to avoid. We seek out founders and colleagues who have learned to simply love the climb. They see it as an endless challenge, a constant state of exertion where the act of climbing is the reward, and the peak is always just out of sight. This mindset produces breakthrough results.

The best version of each of us can learn this and apply it everywhere. It eventually leads to discomfort with the absence of discomfort. Anything we do should summon a fear of failure, otherwise the thing isn't worth doing. From this perspective, dynamic leaders look for mountains, they seek out the very circumstances that put others off. They grow accustomed to criticism and learn to push through the fear, constantly iterating and benefitting from the knowledge it produces.

This chapter is itself a demonstration of the principle. It either worked for you or it didn't. Our aim was to be clear enough and succinct enough that the point could be understood and then applied or rejected. We arrived here through a combination of destination, design, and optimization. By leaving everything else out, we run the risk of failure and rejection but through a willingness to face that risk, we hold the possibility of making a difference for you. Anything else would fall short of our purpose and invalidate the exercise.

Consider yourself, your relationships, your work: where do you lack a destination? How does that show up in design? Where do you find it impossible to optimize? Attack these areas to accelerate success and failure. Both will serve you in your journey to whatever you want to create.

Everything else will hold you back.

CHAPTER TWENTY NINE

Performance/Empowerment/ Competition

We're old enough to remember life before TikTok. Life before Facebook. Life before smartphones. Life before (gasp) widespread use of mobile phones, even the dumb ones. And while this accurately and distressingly dates us, it leaves us with memories of some very interesting circumstances that our younger colleagues find totally unrelatable. Back in the days before mobile phones, you would make plans with friends and sometimes someone wouldn't show up. And then you just didn't know where they were. It was a real and unsolvable mystery. Oftentimes we would just proceed with whatever we had in mind, discover the missing friend later, and learn the explanation.

If these mysteries only occurred before you were born, consider the plot points of any movie or TV show from the eighties or nineties and you'll see what I mean. Countless hours of popular entertainment hinged on mistakes and unknowns that today would be totally unthinkable. This is not nostalgia—we very much enjoy never getting lost and quickly finding the lyrics to any song—but it serves as a reminder as to how performance, as we have defined it, impacts interpersonal relationships.

We define **performance** as purposeful action, aimed at a specific outcome, exposed to analysis to determine its value. In considering its connection to empowerment and competition, it can be instructive to think about performance in simpler terms: simply showing up. Back in the pre-cell phone stone age, you had to count on people to act predictably in order to do anything with them. If we made plans to meet at 8 p.m., you really had to be there for the plans to occur. There was often no other way to reach each other last minute to reschedule, make excuses, explain why you would be late, etc. People who habitually no-showed stopped getting invited. They couldn't be counted on and caused confusion. Their non-performance showed up in a way that doomed the possibility of doing anything together and therefore we stopped trying.

Today, in a constantly connected world of instant communication, there is always an explanation for not showing up. There are reasons, factors, circumstances seemingly beyond anyone's control. In reality, our omnipresent ability to communicate only obscures the same fundamental dynamic. We've all formed relationships with people whose performance fell below the standard where collaboration was possible, despite the fact we knew where they were and why they "couldn't make it this time."

Performance is integrity (keeping your word whole and complete) in action—saying you'll be somewhere at 8 p.m. and taking the necessary steps to be there by that time. It is absolutely necessary to produce **empowerment**, the force multiplier to any team or organization. It is impossible to empower someone else if you yourself occur to them as someone that can't be counted on or present in a way that is consistent and effective.

From a place of performance, we gain access to empowerment. This is where performance can be redirected from individual aims toward collective potential. And this brings us to a critical choice—focus on individual outcomes vs. the possibility of something greater that can only be achieved with a team. Many, many high-performing professionals pause at this juncture and choose, consciously or unconsciously, to avoid the responsibilities of empowerment and team leadership. In some instances, this is due to circumstances that constrain an individual's time or resources that could be channeled into serving others. In others, the choice is driven by fear. In any case, empowering others is required to accomplish anything of real significance. Given a willingness to tackle something big and worthwhile necessitates teamwork and brings us into the realm of competition.

In team sports, the beginning of a match is, by definition, also the end. It represents the conclusion of preparation, practice, and planning. It is the termination of everything done in order to win and now all that is left is **competition**. The clock ticks down, the points count, the result is imminent. In many cases, the outcome appears certain soon after the game begins. One side appears coordinated, committed, and in control. The other is in an accelerating state of disarray, scrambling to react and forced to conform to the other team's style and strategy.

Once the game has begun, it is too late.

When we look at the connection between performance, empowerment, and competition, it is useful to consider this moment of realization. Sport is a limited but useful metaphor. It presents us with perfect tests between two sides operating under the same rules and governed by identical outcomes. Within it, we can see an important dynamic at play.

In team sports, we're often confronted with the paradox of immensely talented individual performers that somehow do not make an effective team. Everyone on the field is a proven winner, superior to all but a few competitors and unquestionably qualified to play their role on the team. This is evidence that performance without empowerment shows up as disaster in competition.

At this point you may be wondering why we don't talk about the concept of teamwork here or anywhere else in the book. It is referenced as an outcome from some of the ideas discussed but never addressed directly. It's a perfectly useful word and we love to see teams in action together, supporting one another and achieving collective goals. However, we have found that effective teamwork, however you choose to define it, hinges specifically on the concepts we're connecting in this chapter. Performance produces the possibility for empowerment and that dynamic, in a competitive context, produces something you would describe as teamwork.

Seeking to establish a working team without focusing on the individual responsibilities of performance and empowerment will create sub-optimal results. This is where we get confused about common goals, shared resources, mutual affinity, and a desire to help each other. While these are all commendable attributes, they don't necessarily add up to very much on their own.

Our view of the sequence goes as follows: one individual commits themselves to a rigorous standard of performance. This is integrity in action and has them occurring for others as consistent, reliable, proficient, and someone with whom significant objectives could be achieved. From here, the high performer helps a colleague discover a new role, become proficient through consistent support, and earn the trust and freedom to eventually perform on their own.

This sequence not only expands the potential of the pair, but also models the means of empowerment so that it can be duplicated without the involvement of the originator. From here, broader coordination is required to guide the empowering growth of the team. In time, numerous key roles are filled and a web of trusting relationships emerges. These bonds that weave across the team are what we usually mean when we use the word "teamwork."

Competition is where we prove out the strength and resilience of the team. After all, the effort required to empower others at scale demands a worthy goal. The team should be doing something that matters, something measurable, and something that holds the possibility of failure. Competition is the test of the team and offers invaluable feedback on gaps, weaknesses, and areas for further consideration.

Throughout the sequence, individual commitment to performance is what drives results. We empower others so that they can do things on their own, without help or intervention. This is the final challenge of the performance/empowerment/ competition combination. Can you trust someone else with a critical responsibility when it matters most? Can they trust you to step up and handle your responsibilities? Can we operate separate-but-together, united in our goal but aligned in ways that don't have us barging into each other's areas of expertise?

Team building relies on two powerful forces: the will to produce performance in yourself and the trust to allow others to perform on your behalf. At first glance, these may seem like contradictory or at least highly distinct exercises. In truth, both feel pretty unnatural at first. Our instinct is to limit our own performance out of fear for the responsibility that comes with it and to mistrust others, fearing that they will be irresponsible with our desires.

It's the same dilemma, only in the reverse, and it produces very limited results. The key here is to override the fear-driven instinct and push through to performance for yourself and others.

In the pre-cell phone era, friendship groups were defined by the folks who showed up. Being a part of the fun required you to understand the plan and be where you were supposed to be at a given time. To our way of thinking, things haven't really changed that much. You might have 1,000 para-social relationships, a few hundred folks you communicate with through "likes" or "follows", a couple dozen in your contacts that get the occasional text or emoji. And then you have your squad—your team—the friends you count on to show up. Your performance opens up the opportunity to empower each other and this, in turn, makes things happen.

With or without your phones.

CHAPTER THIRTY

Objectivity/Joy/Curiosity

Spoiler alert: this chapter ends with an admonishment to discover your own path with an open mind, a joyful spirit, and a constant sense of curiosity.

Whoops, sorry about that!

In the age of the internet, we find it harder to avoid information than to acquire it. When seemingly all knowledge is available at all times, it can be exceedingly difficult to ignore the final score of a game you missed, the twist at the end of the new show you haven't watched yet, or the day-to-day performance of a stock you once believed in but are now starting to doubt. These are spoilers, the information that robs you of the joy we find in discovering something for ourselves in real time.

In these simple examples, we can clearly see the value in not already knowing something. It even leads us to warn friends not to tell us things or to stay off Twitter in a desperate attempt to protect it. Part of the rush in getting surprised is the sense that there is so little surprise in other parts of our lives that we cherish the moments where it can occur. This is an illusion, of course, our lives are full of surprises, but most of us interpret these events as part of a pattern we already knew or confirmation of what we long suspected and this is a problem.

In our chapter on **objectivity** (*see also* pages 31–5), we took pains to explain the dangers of a judgmental mindset. Judgment provides answers from previously held beliefs. These beliefs enable us to predict and explain anything, spoiling every story before it begins.

Consider the reasons why you picked up this book. There is something happening for you around the possibility of creation or perhaps the hope of getting unstuck. There is something you can see for yourself that you want or hope to make possible. Now think of all the reasons why you won't actually do it.

You can't really raise money for a startup. After all, you can't take on that risk, not with all your responsibilities and obligations. Even if you did, you don't know how to build a team or run a company. This book is fine and all but most of it doesn't apply to you anyways. Better to stay the course and do what you know how to do.

Beneath all of that is something else—the judgment that justifies what you are doing and reconciles your place in the world through beliefs about what is right and wrong, good and bad. For some of you, this might go back to the economic circumstances of your family and the sense that rich people are intrinsically bad and that doing something that might make you rich is gross and unethical. Others might hold beliefs about race or gender, about the kinds of people you might have to interact with in order to make something significant, about what you owe to your family that would preclude you from making a change in your life. In short, you can see something in front of you and you move away from it with a series of explanations. These explanations are founded in judgments that justify your actions and make it okay to be what you already are, and so you remain.

Our point is that many of you seem to already know what is coming next. You are your own spoilers, ruining the twist before the show even starts. Worst of all, it seems impossible to avoid this dynamic inside your own head. You can't turn off Twitter notifications inside your brain. You already know it in the instant it occurs, an automatic cycle of seeing the future as a means of justifying the present. This is the limitation of judgment and only an objective mindset can break through to new possibilities.

Once you take hold of a values-neutral, non-judgmental perspective, even in one small area of your life, you open up the possibility for **joy**. Experiencing something as it is, without needing it to conform with what you believe, allows you to learn and grow in all new ways. It fosters appreciation for people where otherwise you might have felt fear or resentment. It keeps you learning, keeps you grounded, and makes you more present for anyone with whom you hope to connect or collaborate. This is available to you in your work and your overall ambitions for life and once you see it, your access to joy in what you do will increase exponentially.

Being open to new things and not already knowing what they mean before they occur creates access to joy. From here, we can live in a world of **curiosity**, the necessary condition for the breakthroughs we need in work and life. This is especially critical because our access to curiosity naturally diminishes as we age. Philosopher and psychologist Alison Gopnik compares the consciousness of a baby to a lantern, with interest and curiosity distributed in all directions to maximize learning. This phenomenon is familiar to any parent who has attempted to dress a small child and been constantly thwarted by a thousand (seemingly) meaningless distractions. Children harvest information indiscriminately, always exploring in service of a rapidly developing brain. As we age, Gopnik compares our consciousness to a spotlight—tightly focused on the goal or action we've defined for ourselves. This helps us be productive (someone has to focus on dressing the child) but far less curious. We learn less and become more rigid over time.

This natural process, coupled with our desire to avoid risk, can turn any of us into joyless, incurious know-it-alls. And while we see risk in a life driven by powerful curiosity, consider the dangers of living inside of one's self-limiting beliefs. Never attempting to raise funds for a startup is no better than trying and failing, the only difference is that you miss out on the experience. Keeping your job for fear of the financial instability of self-employment could prove immensely costly—what if you became a smashing success? Committing yourself to a promising new collaboration holds some risk of disappointment, but the alternative guarantees less fulfillment, less impact, less fun.

An objective, curious mindset also produces very different experiences with others. We've all had instances where someone engaged us in conversation, not to truly learn our perspective but to find out if we would endorse theirs. Commitment to predictive beliefs and judgments limit what we get back from others as they experience us as being closed or already decided. Being present and curious produces something very different—a sense of being heard and a greater possibility for co-creation. This dynamic, when applied consistently, can have far-reaching implications for any leader and team.

Judgment robs you of curiosity and being experienced by others as a curious person. Objectivity creates access to curiosity, a joyful state of being that is attractive and influential. We'll leave it up to you to decide which approach carries the most risk. We encourage you to discover your own path with an open mind, a joyful spirit, and a constant sense of curiosity.

CHAPTER THIRTY ONE

Focus/Story/Connection

Most movie scripts are full of heartbreaking decisions for the screenwriter. There simply isn't time to showcase all the characters they want. Scenes that don't directly contribute to the narrative arc of the story have to be cut. In order for the audience respond with emotion to the story—to connect—the writer has to bring maniacal **focus** to the script.

This focus is most evident in the logline, the one-sentence disruption that sells the screenplay. For example: "A 17-year-old aristocrat falls in love with a kind but poor artist aboard the luxurious, ill-fated R.M.S. *Titanic.*" While it doesn't quite conjure an image of Leo DiCaprio holding Kate Winslet's arms out on the prow of the ship, all the essentials of the **story** are there. Every Hollywood movie was at one point merely a logline, a short thread of information that the filmmaker brings to life.

We emphasize focus because the act of storytelling seems to set off every impulse *besides* focus. We tell stories to ourselves and others to find connection and meaning in the experiences we share. And in doing so, we ramble. We go off on tangents. We include meaningless detail. Like artists neglecting the boundaries of the canvas, we splash paint all over the wall in hopes that the sheer mass of color will intrigue the audience. Sadly, it does not.

Storytelling is a meaningful concept to anyone committed to creating something and it requires focus to ensure the story achieves its aim. A lack of focus is unproductive at best and usually harmful. Here's where most storytellers go wrong:

1) Assuming that the story will tell itself. Hardworking founders and leaders tend to shun the spotlight and avoid anything that looks like attracting credit or attention to themselves. This mindset, while commendable in its intention, can lead to the misperception that storytelling itself is unnecessary. The performance of the company or team will be the story and no further narrative is needed. In reality, persistent connection is impossible to achieve without a story that gives meaning to what is happening. Leaders have a responsibility to tell the story of what they are up to and if they avoid it, fall victim to someone's else version.

2) Using story to explain instead of inspire. This is where leaders attempt to own a narrative by deconstructing the chain of events that led to every key decision. The story becomes a documentary, a historical record more concerned with "getting it right" than communicating what it feels like to be a part of the company or the idea. While it's important to maintain a clear perspective on the events that led up to the moment, that archive of information is not story. It informs without inspiring and in doing so, leaves audiences cold.

3) Letting enthusiasm overrun focus. Excited about their ideas and the teams they've assembled, leaders are vulnerable to messy, convoluted narratives that become hard to follow. Moments of real emotional resonance are undermined by a lack of clarity or coherent progression toward a defined goal. Unfocused storytelling can be joyful and entertaining, but it is ultimately doomed by sheer illegibility.

The first important act of storytelling for any leader is the narrative they tell themselves. Each of us is the star of our own movies—so what is your logline? Our idea of personal storytelling is distinct from delusion or mindlessly positive self-talk. It should be real and grounded but link the events of your life in a way that produces narrative quality. What does your character want? What are the obstacles in front of them? How can you have an audience understand and engage with the plot?

The second act is the story you tell friends, funders, and collaborators in hopes of working with them to make something happen. This is you literally telling your story, the interpersonal communication of the plot and the point. With discipline and focus, the story should sound roughly the same to each of them and gain resonance with repetition. Good stories are easy to remember and fun to share—yours should spark the first instances of second-hand repetition, a way for your story to live outside of you.

Finally, as you gather momentum toward your goal and move through your story in action, your focus shifts to a way of enabling others to share and be part of the story. This is where story scales in service of the idea, where *your* story becomes *the* story and acts as a powerful tool to connect with clients, customers, and other audiences. This is not to say the story is all about you. In fact, as time goes on, you will take on a smaller role in service of the larger narrative. When shared with focus, story can create **connection**. That connection speeds the distance to collaboration, fundraising, customer acquisition, and more.

CHAPTER THIRTY TWO

Power/Urgency/Transparency

In the original 1993 adaptation of *Jurassic Park*, an exasperated Dr. Ian Malcolm argues with park proprietor John Hammond over the wisdom of bringing dinosaurs back to life. "Your scientists were so preoccupied with whether or not they could," he exclaims, "that they didn't stop to think if they should." The mega-blockbuster begat five sequels over the next 20 years, itself becoming an ironic example of the same hubris Malcolm was bemoaning. Nevertheless, his complaint still resonates.

The original *Jurassic Park* story, first conceived by writer Michael Crichton, wrestles with moral and ethical questions that arise when brilliant people come together to create something without fully exploring its consequences (and also dinosaurs run around and do cool stuff). Enamored with the notion of creating living, breathing dinosaurs for public viewing, Hammond and his team never took the time to consider what would happen when species separated by millennia collide at the same time and place.

This may seem like a strange place to begin a discussion on the connection between power, urgency, and transparency but this combination confronts us with some deeper questions around the meaning of what we do and the legacy we hope to leave. Harnessing power as we have defined it often produces urgency. These elements, when made public through transparent demonstration of the work in action, can produce dramatic and lasting results. Note that we simply used the word "results" without classifying them as good or bad.

As you may have noticed by now, we've taken great care throughout this book to talk through each concept without assigning value judgments to anything. This is very intentional and our reasoning becomes obvious in the chapter on objectivity (*see also* pages 31–5). Moreover, our aim is to spark others into action and productivity, not to dictate the right kind of productivity or presume that others would share our perspective on what ought or ought not to be done. Judgment impedes access to learning and makes challenging concepts all the more difficult to understand. This is not to say that we lack moral or ethical perspectives. Far from it. It simply means that those considerations are better served in a book with a different purpose, but when we consider this particular combination of concepts, we must acknowledge the possibilities involved.

Power, as we have defined it, begins with seeing everything as a possibility. It means opening yourself up to the immense potential you possess and acting into that potential to make something happen. **Urgency** is the maximum speed of productive progress, an action state defined by commitment, motivation, and enthusiasm. Finally, **transparency** is understood to be operating in a way that has internal and external audiences understand your perspective and see your work in action. This is the communication piece that brings your power and urgency into the public sphere, where it can influence others and generate connection with the outside world.

This sequence is especially notable in that it often comes together naturally, without conscience consideration or a specific desire to do so. Effective deployment of power produces urgency and in doing so, an impulse to have others notice and be a part of what is being created. Working together, these concepts build momentum for whatever is underway and act as a propulsive force. Whatever the destination, it fuels the engines and speeds leaders and teams on their course. While power + urgency + transparency can build an Apple Computers, it can also build a Jurassic Park.

This is where you may find yourself feeling as though we're being a bit dramatic. After all, who is actually trying to bring dinosaurs back to life? What is the danger? We would encourage you to consider your own interpretation of all the statements in this book that reference doing something big, significant, meaningful, or lasting. The potential we see in every person to create change. If you read that to be euphemistic or hyperbolic, we would encourage you to revisit chapters from section one, such as Leadership, Power, or Purpose, but this time take them at face value. Read them as though we meant everything we said. Seeing your potential as small or your potential impact as insignificant says something about how you see yourself. It shows the limitations of the power you grant yourself to act and create.

Misalignment between expectation and reality can produce a dangerous dynamic, one where the perceived responsibility for what you create lags the size and impact of the thing itself. In *Jurassic Park*, Hammond only came to appreciate his mistakes when the dinosaurs were literally chasing his grandchildren. Only when his immediate family was threatened did he truly consider the consequences to others. Sadly, this delayed realization effect plays out in real life over and over. We're using a Hollywood movie as an example in this chapter not because we lack real world alternatives, we chose it because it is clear, concise, and politically neutral.

Creating and scaling a business requires leaders to engage in healthcare, public policy, environmental impact, and more, all with massive social and cultural implications. Building product means enabling people to do something and therefore you will hold responsibility with what is done with the product you create. There are layers and layers of responsibility to consider, along with the bigger question of how you want to be remembered, how your own children and grandchildren may perceive your influence on the world.

So, what do we do about this? How can we avoid the dangers that come with unleashing power, urgency, and transparency? The first and most important step is to see and take seriously the power you possess to change the world around you. This unlocks any number of other concepts but in this context, it serves to build your sense of responsibility and keep you ahead of delayed realization. Accepting that you *could* do something offers space to consider whether or not you *should*.

Secondly, consider your motivation. Most entrepreneurs are driven in part by the desire to prove someone wrong. While this can be useful, it must be recognized and balanced with your desire to serve others, solve a problem, or make life easier. You can absolutely stick it to the haters while still doing good—they are not mutually exclusive.

Thirdly, don't wait for the dinosaurs to chase your grandchildren in order to ponder your legacy. Your perspective on lasting impact will change as you age and will certainly take on new dimensions if or when you have children. But anyone can imagine their future children, consider the lives of their friends and neighbors, and be mindful of what you would want someone to say at your funeral. Legacy will matter more as time goes on but you can serve your future self by taking action now to ensure you don't live with regret later on.

Finally, embrace the finite nature of your ability to create. Your time is limited. If your mindset is informed by what you can accumulate to yourself, the recognition you can earn, the energy and affirmation you want for yourself, you'll find it difficult to operate with optimal responsibility and care. This mindset will shrink your capacity to collaborate with others and grow your incentive to focus on what you can do, not what you should do. Seeing yourself in a continuum of creation, the inheritor of those that came before you and the steward of something for those that follow, will serve your decision-making and drive you to a destination free of regret.

We set out to write a book to inspire. More than that, we wrote this to spark action, to have readers not only think but act and create. Within that, we're present to our own responsibility. It's entirely possible that someone could read this book, find use in it, and create something dangerous or damaging. We acknowledge that possibility and take responsibility for it. Having said that, the opportunity to contribute to someone else's positive creation is too important not to run the risk. It is tempting to tell ourselves that this book won't matter much—not many people will read it, no one would actually translate these concepts into harmful action, etc. And then we would be in the delayed realization of responsibility doom loop, staring bewildered at the dinosaurs rampaging around the park. Therefore, we have truly considered not just what we could do, but whether or not we should.

The rest is up to you.

Index